THE STRANGE CASE
OF DR. TERRY AND MR. CHIMES

Terry Chimes

Published by:

WP Wilkinson Publishing Pty Ltd ACN 006 042 173
Level 4, 2 Collins Street, Melbourne, Vic 3000
Tel: 613 9654 5446, www.wilkinsonpublishing.com.au

National Library of Australia Cataloguing-in-Publication data:

Author:	Chimes, Terry, author.
Title:	The strange case of Dr Terry and Mr Chimes / Terry Chimes.
ISBN:	9781922178244 (paperback)
Subjects:	Chimes, Terry.
	Rock musicians--Great Britain--Biography.
	Chiropractors--Great Britain--Biography.
	Counselors--Great Britain--Biography.
Dewey Number:	782.42164092
Cover Design:	Milan Jovanovic
Layout:	Chris Georgiou

THE STRANGE CASE OF DR TERRY AND MR CHIMES is also available as an eBook.

PREFACE

Some people only ever have one ambition in life. Others, like myself, have several. Inside me there have always been two people, each trying to dominate. Dr Terry wanted to learn about health and disease and heal people. Mr Chimes wanted to spend his time on a stage and live the life of a rock star. Who won the fight? Well, the struggle is not over yet, but what has happened so far and what I have learned and experienced is the substance of this book. Mr Chimes hopes that this book entertains you and Dr Terry hopes that it helps you in some way. We both thank you for reading it.

DEDICATION

This book is dedicated to my late father, Bill Chimes, the man who could do anything and always told his children that they could too.

CONTENTS

ACKNOWLEDGEMENTS

I would like to thank all of the people who have come to see me play or bought the records. Those who have trusted me with their health and those who have sought my advice or attended talks. You have all taught me a great deal and I thank you for that. Thanks to all the friends and relatives who have kindly read early versions and given me valuable feedback, especially The Baker who either has a better memory than I or was less drunk. Thanks to my long-suffering typists Kay Lundy and Annie Sharma – stand by for the next project! Well done to Milan Jovanovic for his striking cover design. I thank Paul D. McCarthy for teaching me about book writing. Robert Lambolle for patiently copy-editing my endless tirades. Sam Wilkinson and Chris Georgiou for the all-important final touches. My agent Rick Mayston (from Getty Images) for finding me people I can work with. My two publishers, Michael Wilkinson and Chris Lascelles for their faith and enthusiasm. To all of you much love and gratitude and I promise to be quicker at writing the next book.

CHAPTER I
A STRANGE CHILD

"Often people attempt to live their lives backwards; they try to have more things, or more money, in order to do more of what they want, so they will be happier. The way it actually works is the reverse. You must first be who you really are, then do what you need to do, in order to have what you want."

Margaret Young

In 1989 I announced to the world that I was giving up playing music to go off and study full time. Most people reacted in a way I would have expected had I told them I was about to go and have a sex change operation. If they had read the book that you are about to read, they would have understood perfectly.

I grew up in the East End of London. This was, and still is, one of the poorest areas in the country – but it's very special. The people there are different. They even have their own way of speaking in Cockney rhyming slang. Don't worry – this book is in plain English.

I am the middle one of three brothers, which is supposed to make me a good communicator. There was a fourth, the eldest, but he was stillborn. He was named Billy after my father. Apparently, if my mum had given birth twenty times there would have been twenty boys. We grew up living a stone's throw away from numerous uncles, aunties and cousins. Despite living in a poor area, we never wanted for anything and enjoyed growing up in a loving and close family. I was a very happy child who loved to daydream.

Dr Terry was the first side to appear at that innocent time in my life. I loved nature. Plants were fascinating and animals were incredibly exciting to me. My childhood was a constant quest to acquire more pets. I remember, as a 12-year-old, being woken up at 3 am by my older brother John, who was most displeased to have been disturbed by my hamster trotting across his neck. Apart from pets, dead animals also fascinated me. My Uncle, Manny, was a driver for a meat company. He would give me various bits of animals, such as eyes and hearts, for me to dissect at home. Since none of the rest of the family shared my interest in these specimens, I now realise how tolerant they were of my strange habits.

However, my mother, Donna Chimes, found herself somewhat lacking in tolerance when she walked into our lounge and found me, at the age of four, chopping up worms on the arm of the sofa. I still maintain that she was quite unreasonable about the whole affair. It got worse. When I was six, I was delighted to find a frog in the garden (this was the East End, where frogs were comparatively rare). There was only one problem: the frog appeared to be dead. I had read about this amphibian habit called winter hibernation. I thought that if I warmed up the frog he might come back to life and I would have a pet. So I did what any reasonable person would have done. I popped him in the oven and turned it up full. Ovens take some time to warm up and, as a six year old, I had a very short attention span, so I went off to my room to play with some toys. It was my mother who first noticed the smoke coming from the kitchen. Mothers are amazingly clever, aren't they? As soon as she found that frog, she knew exactly who put it there!

I don't remember my first day at school but my mother has since reminded me of it. She was concerned that I wouldn't like going to school and had asked me at the end of my first day what it was like. Apparently I replied, "It's alright but I don't think I'll bother going tomorrow". She told me that if I didn't go tomorrow another boy would take my place and I wouldn't be able to go again, so, reluctantly, I agreed to try one more day.

A few days later, I was desperate for the toilet in the playground at school but I didn't know where it was, so I simply urinated into the drain. A

few minutes later two girls dragged the teacher over towards me and pointed at me accusingly saying, "it was him" and I got a severe smacking on the legs. I distinctly remember looking at those girls and thinking, "whatever have I done to you that you would do this to me?" I am no opponent of corporal punishment but I think they could have at least shown me where the toilet was.

Around this time I asked my mother about cigarettes, and she amazed me by asking if I would like to try one. This surprised me, as I knew she hated smoking. I agreed to try it and she lit up one of my father's cigarettes for me. I inhaled really hard and immediately ran to the nearest water tap. It felt like my lungs were on fire. That cigarette had the desired effect and I never tried it again.

My paternal grandmother died when I was six. I wasn't told anything about this. Presumably they thought I was too young. One day I casually asked my father why we hadn't seen her lately. He replied, "She's in heaven." I knew all about heaven from school and so I simply said, "Oh, ok," and thought no more of it.

My maternal grandmother was a very central figure in the family, not least because her descendents seem to have populated half the East End of London. On her 85th birthday celebration the large hall was full of people and my Uncle Manny said to her, "Do you realise that all of the people in this room have come from you?" She would often tell stories about her early life, which had been very hard. At the age of 10 her father died and she had to be put into a workhouse, somewhat similar to the one in *Oliver Twist*. Her hair hung almost down to her waist – this was cut off in one fell swoop as she entered the workhouse. They worked from 7 am until 6 pm six days a week. I found that story quite shocking. Not because hair was that important but because she had absolutely no control over her life at that time. That story and others like it made me determined to have some degree of control over my own life. This is why, from quite an early age, I always looked carefully at different career paths to make sure that I made the right choice. I wanted control over my life and I wanted to do something I enjoyed. Some would say that since my Gran was born in the 19th century it was impossible to compare that with the time I grew up – the Swinging Sixties. I didn't agree.

My two uncles, Manny and Billy, were always around when I was growing up. They bore an uncanny resemblance to the Kray Twins (the infamous East London gangsters of the sixties), but were actually the most charming men you could ever meet. They worked really hard loading meat onto lorries, driving the lorries to their destination and then unloading them. I remember looking at the cows and sheep hanging on hooks in the back of their lorries and marvelling at the sheer scale of the job of lifting these enormous beasts, one after another. What I found shocking about all of this is that my uncles worked incredibly hard; they hated their work and got paid very little for it. Of course, you had to admire them for getting up every morning and doing a job they hated so that their families would always be provided for. Furthermore, they were both extremely cheerful when you met them socially. Perhaps it was my tendency towards vegetarianism (more about that later) that particularly made me feel appalled by the work they had to do. For me this was ample evidence that you need to think very carefully about what you do for a living. At the age of 13 I promised myself that I would find something to do that I enjoyed and I would never do a job I hated – life was way too short for that. These childhood experiences heavily influenced my choices later in life.

Kids growing up in the East End tend to have low expectations about life. I saw this all around me as a child and it can still be seen there to this day. However, this did not apply to us – my father made sure of that.

To say that my dad, Bill Chimes, was a one-off would be an understatement. I meet all sorts of people in my life but I don't ever expect to meet anyone like him again. He was 5' 5" and 3/8ths – a figure he often quoted to us. He was a dedicated family man with absolutely no interest in boozing or gambling. He had a gift of meticulous attention to detail combined with the patience of a saint – qualities I have unfortunately failed to inherit. He worked for the *Sunday Times Magazine*, making photographic plates for printing colour pictures. This was a highly skilled craftsman's job back then. As a child I would boast to my friends that my dad could do anything because it seemed to me he could. He always seemed to have the answer to virtually any

question you asked. He could strip down and rebuild any engine, repair any domestic appliance and was a wizard at electronics. He even created a series of animated films with a cine camera featuring the toys we used to play with.

When I was 10 a friend of mine had one of those model cars – a Dinky. It broke in half and all and sundry told him that it would be impossible to repair such a thing. They were basically right because these toys were made of die-cast zinc, which cannot be soldered or welded. However, whenever my dad heard the words "it can't be done" he would immediately set about doing it. Sure enough, when I told him about my friend's car he told him to bring it to him. He cut a thread into both halves of the broken car and screwed each half onto the same piece of stud so that they met in the middle. He then filled the tiny gap between the two halves, sanded it smooth and repainted the whole car. The finished article looked brand new. This experience, along with numerous others, confirmed to me that my dad really could do anything.

The other thing to say about my dad was that he was obsessed with music. He played the saxophone and clarinet. He had had his own dance band, even making a couple of records in his younger days. He couldn't go professional because of the needs of his young family but I think it pleased him a great deal to see his three sons earn their living through music. Sons will often adopt the values of their fathers. I have many friends who became crazy about sport because their fathers were. My father never cared about sport, and nor do any of us, but we are all crazy about music! My dad's brother, my uncle Pat, is also a dedicated musician. He played the trumpet, and his son, Tim Chimes, who is about my age, plays the saxophone in swing bands.

During World War II my dad was in the Royal Air Force, stationed in Aden on the Arabian Peninsula. His job was to repair Spitfire engines (the fighter planes of choice during World War II). If you were a pilot flying one of those planes in mortal combat, you would definitely want someone like my dad making sure the engine was working properly.

When I was eight years old I was in conversation with my father, discussing what I would be when I grew up, and he came up with an astonishing

statement: "You can be anything you want." I quickly decided that this was nonsense and in order to disprove the idea I said, "Well I couldn't become the Prime Minister of England, could I?" I sat back waiting for him to concede defeat but to my amazement he said, "Absolutely. You can be Prime Minister. But you would have to want it and work really hard for it." I walked away scratching my head and wondering if this could really be true. I did not want to be Prime Minister but that was not the point. The effect of this little exchange would not be seen until much later, when I was nineteen years old and looking for a band I could play in.

It was also when I was eight that the Beatles burst onto the scene in a way never seen before or since. Looking at those four young men on the stage convinced me that being in a famous band would be a good career choice for someone who could "do anything you want!" As Beatlemania soared, our family had a nice surprise. My uncle, Harry Boy, turned up one day with Beatles jackets for me and for my older brother, John. These were exact replicas of the collarless jackets that the Beatles were wearing and they were not yet available in the shops. As an eight year old I didn't really see what the big deal was but people kept stopping me in the street begging to know where I got the jacket. Of course, I just told them that my uncle got it for me, which was of no use to them whatsoever. Incidentally, none of us ever really figured out what Harry Boy did for a living. He was rather like the TV comedy character Del Boy in *Only Fools and Horses.*

We grew up near a car breakers yard. My friend Tommy and I spotted, amongst all the junk, a real sword – one actually made of metal. We already had plastic swords but this was way more exciting. It occurred to the two of us that if we took it no one would really miss it – or so we told ourselves. So we hatched a plan. I would run to the other end of the yard to distract the vicious German Shepherd guarding the place while Tommy would pull the sword out. The plan worked and we were now the proud possessors of this sword, although we hadn't discussed who would keep it once we had it. This was an early insight for me into the perils of partnerships. I went to bed that night thinking that what I had actually done was stealing. My Catholic upbringing

told me that stealing was a sin and an offence to God. I felt very bad about it and wasn't sure what to do. I felt that I should give it back, but Tommy had no such qualms of conscience.

I was quite upset at the time and my parents asked me several times what was wrong but I never told them. In the end I took the problem to the priest at Confession. He told me off, made me promise not to do it again and gave me some homework to do. After doing my homework, I felt as if a huge weight had been lifted from my shoulders and I never wanted to have that feeling of a bad conscience again. So despite the criticisms you hear about a Catholic upbringing and the concept of Confession, in my particular case, at the time, it worked well.

When I was nine and Bryn, my younger brother, was four we started to play music together. I had a recorder and he had a drum. We couldn't produce anything elaborate but what we did do was get used to playing with someone else. In all the years I taught people to play music I found that one of the biggest challenges was to get them to listen to the other musicians they played with.

My dad had the occasional habit of coming home with a surprise gift, such as a pair of pet rabbits or a new gadget. One day he presented us with a reel-to-reel tape recorder. We'd never seen anything like it before and our friends certainly hadn't. It meant we could record music and play it back, which was quite mind-blowing at the time. It also allowed us to record speech. It had a microphone with a stop-start switch built in. John, my older brother, and I couldn't resist the temptation to incriminate my long-suffering mother. We interviewed her with a long series of questions but by careful use of the on/off button, switched all the answers. For instance, we asked her, "Do you ever steal anything?", turned off the microphone when she said "No", and with the off button still pressed, ask her if she lived in London and turn the microphone back on for her "Yes" answer. So after an apparently harmless interview of 20 questions we had taped evidence of her admitting to all manner of crimes! But the real blessing of that recorder was that we could tape ourselves playing music and hear what it sounded like. This facility is considered essential now for any developing musician but back in those days most kids didn't have it.

At the age of ten I was active, with John, in the local scout troop. They were putting on a play called *Rival Brothers*. John accepted the role of the older brother and they offered me the lead role as the younger brother. They told me to think about it and decide whether I wanted to do it. I thought "if he can do it, so can I," and so I agreed. I've sometimes wondered if my life would have turned out differently had I said no. We rehearsed for many weeks and eventually co-stared in a show that involved singing and acting in front of an audience. Funny that it was called Rival Brothers as we both ended up earning our living as musicians, both actually playing drums – albeit in a very different way. I found that I enjoyed performing on a stage and never felt nervous about it. This absence of nerves before performing lasted my whole career, which was very handy. In later life, so many of my musician colleagues were nervous wrecks when they were about to perform.

I would attend Scouts every Friday night. As I didn't live near the school, I would go to my uncle Manny's house for dinner. I did this regularly for years. Manny and his wife Joan always made me feel so welcome. Soon after I joined the scouts, Richard Tillbrook was appointed scout leader. He would only have been about 18 at the time and was new to his leadership role but he brought a lot of enthusiasm, working way beyond the call of duty. Richard went on to become a teacher of great influence and we always joked that he was like Mr Chips from the movie, *Goodbye Mr Chips*. He later retrained for the priesthood and now runs a parish in Colchester. Richard and I will remain friends for the rest of our lives.

My mum has an older sister called Kitty who is a great character. Kitty was always full of life and you could guarantee she would be willing to try any sporting activity with any person, at any time. This would include snooker, football, go-kart racing and even boxing. Kitty had a market stall selling ladies' underwear. As I reached the age of 10, she kindly gave me a job. I had only one duty to perform, which was to stand at the stall and watch everybody, raising the alarm should there be any theft. The stall consisted of a huge pile of ladies' underwear of all sorts of colours, most of which at the time appeared to me to be much too large to fit an elephant, let alone a woman.

The customers would walk up and spend ages sifting through the underwear and then either buy something or simply leave. Kitty informed me that many of the women would slip something into their bag while she wasn't looking and walk off.

I started the day determined to apprehend any thieves, diligently watching every single customer for signs of foul play. Unfortunately for Kitty, my boredom threshold at that age was between one and two minutes. Inevitably I started daydreaming. It seems as a security person I was as much use as a chocolate teapot. Kitty was a very generous person and paid me for my day's work (in actuality, two minutes' work). I felt very elated at the thought of having earned my own money and being able to spend it on what I liked. Shockingly, I was never invited back for further surveillance work but I will always be grateful to Kitty for starting me off.

During my childhood I did all kinds of jobs to earn extra money such as cleaning cars, gardening or running errands. Every 5th November I would go out to try and raise money by asking "a penny for the guy". For the benefit of non-British readers, Guy Fawkes was a Catholic revolutionary who, in 1605, very nearly succeeded in blowing up the Houses of Parliament while it was being opened by the King. Possibly one of the earliest known terrorists, he was caught and subsequently hanged. Since that time countless British children construct an effigy of Guy Fawkes, which is burned on a bonfire during firework displays on 5th November. A couple of days before, children proudly display their Guy Fawkes effigies and ask passers by to donate a penny for their efforts. Some parents disapproved, regarding this as begging, in the same way that some parents disapprove of trick or treat on Halloween. I saw this as an excellent business opportunity and went a step further by doing some market research. Having experimented with different sites we discovered that easily the best way to raise money was to set up outside the local hospital at visiting time. Visitors would be in a very sympathetic state of mind, manifested in generosity towards any children who happened to be there. This early introduction to the efficacy of market research would prove useful on many further occasions in my life.

The system of education in England at the time was a two-tier set up whereby kids who were considered bright could pass an exam called the 11-plus and would go to a school for higher ability children called a grammar school (a confusing name for Americans). The kids that couldn't pass that exam would go to a less academic institution known as a secondary modern. As I approached the stage when a decision needed to be made, the politicians came up with a new system that they thought would be fairer, the so-called comprehensive school, where children of all abilities would go. There was a battle between the traditionalists and the modernists as far as education was concerned and that battle is still going on today. The upshot for me was that I still took the exam but the teachers didn't tell us it was the 11-plus so as not to put pressure on us. I passed the exam and went on to a grammar school called Raines Foundation. This school had been set up by a rich brewer in the 18th century to give kids from poor areas a high quality education. One of the advantages of going to a grammar school is that they keep telling you how clever you are, which helps negate the natural tendency of children in poor areas to have low expectations. Producing rock stars was probably not the intention of the founder of the school, but increasing self-confidence certainly was.

As a child I never really wanted football boots for Christmas, I tended to go for books, microscopes and chemistry sets. My favourite present when I was about twelve was called The Visible Man. This was a see-through plastic model of a man containing all of the vital organs, each of which could be removed and observed and which you painted yourself. Christmas presents were one area in which Dr Terry managed to get one up on Mr Chimes.

Around this time John started to get seriously interested in classical music. My dad responded by acquiring a high quality Hi-Fi system together with some records. John's favourite was Tchaikovsky's first piano concerto. I'm certain that I can still remember every note of that piece; he played it so many times. He learned to play the piano but made a conscious decision to specialise in timpani or kettledrums. Of course, we didn't have any timpani – they cost thousands of pounds – so John would practice for hours on end using

pillows. He later joined the London Schools Symphony Orchestra, which gave him the chance to get serious about learning. He was quite obsessed with these drums and he certainly learned fast.

At thirteen my passion for nature showed no signs of abating. In 1969, when my friends were buying rock albums, I was thrilled to read that the BBC was releasing an album of recordings of British wild animal noises. This album, unsurprisingly, was not in stock in any of the shops and had to be specially ordered. I can remember the smirking face of the sales assistant as he ordered it. He was clearly thinking, "I've got a right nut on my hands here" – but I didn't care!

My younger brother, Bryn, is a master practitioner of Neuro-Linguistic Programming (NLP). According to NLP there are three sensory modalities or three ways to perceive the world. They are seeing, hearing and touching. What we now know is that most people predominate in one or other of these. In my case, I am an auditory – my sense of hearing is the most important to me. No big shock then to learn that I became a musician. I had read all about wild animals, I had seen pictures of them and I had seen them for real in the zoo (obviously, I was a zoo season ticket holder) but I was desperate to find out what they sounded like, and here was the answer.

Incidentally, if you are an auditory and your wife is a visual, it is quite likely that you spend a lot of time and energy telling her how much you love her, etc. As a visual, she would think this is all very well but where are my flowers or trip to somewhere with a lovely view? Clearly then, it pays to know the primary sensory modality of the person you are dealing with. If you want to know which one you are, there is an easy test: Ask yourself, if you could have hugs from your loved one, or beautiful words, or visual delights such as flowers, but not all three, which one would you choose? When you have answered that question, you will know which type you are!

Over the years of my childhood I had many pets but I was always hankering after something bigger and better. To me, dogs were too ordinary and I wanted something exotic. I decided a mongoose would fit the bill and

after nagging my mother relentlessly we went down to an exotic pet shop in Camden Town. It was located just a few yards from where The Clash would rehearse about six years later. Talking to the man in the shop was very disappointing for me. It seemed that to tame a mongoose you needed to acquire it at a very young age, otherwise it could be quite vicious. The problem was the quarantine laws at that time meant that the young mongoose would have to be imprisoned for 6 months before being allowed through customs. By this time it would be an aggressive adult. It seemed that my plan to have an exotic predator as a pet would have to be abandoned.

However, I was not to be deterred and my research told me that the nearest alternative that could be bred in the UK would be a polecat, which is actually a form of ferret, but black and white in colour. This would not be a wild polecat but one bred in captivity – farmers breed them for hunting rabbits. I arranged to get one upon my return from a sailing trip with the Scouts. While I was away my dad had put his building skills to good use and built a fabulous pen for my new pet. This structure way surpassed my wildest expectations, being about 18 feet long. My polecat would be the happiest animal in London.

I took possession of a young female and called her Venus. The rest of the family were not at all sure this was a good idea but there was no going back now. Whenever I brought Venus into the house the others would retreat to the safety of the lounge, keeping the doors shut and leaving me with the run of the rest of the house. You would think that Venus was a full-grown tiger the way they behaved! I later realised that female polecats need to breed to stay healthy so I persuaded my long-suffering family that we needed to have a family of polecats. We found a male called Arthur who was to be the father of the new family. Arthur would not move in; he would simply come and impregnate Venus. The mating ritual of polecats is one of the most extraordinary things I have ever seen. The male is much larger and stronger. Arthur walked up to Venus, grabbed her by the scruff of the neck and dragged her round and round the enclosure for over an hour whilst she screamed. I had to repeatedly assure my family that I had read about this

and it was all quite normal. They couldn't bear the screams and had to go elsewhere. After completely exhausting his new wife, Arthur then proceeded to go about siring the new litter. This took a further hour. At this point the screams of Venus were truly ear-splitting.

Venus gave birth six weeks later to thirteen young, one of which died very soon after. As anyone would expect, she ate the dead baby (or kit as it's known). This was one step too far for most of my family who asked me not to tell them any more about the breeding of polecats, as they couldn't cope! Of course, from a biological perspective eating the dead offspring is the only safe thing to do. Otherwise you would have a rotting corpse and an infection spreading throughout the litter. This was a fine example of recycling. The other twelve thrived and grew very fast. A few weeks later they went through a very comical stage. The male kits were considerably larger than Venus but still quite young. One by one, all twelve youngsters would leave the safety of the pen to go into the wire netting run. Venus would grab them and drag them back into the safety of the pen. Whilst she was dragging one back, two others would venture out. I was amazed at how relentlessly she continued to keep dragging them back in. After a few days she gave up, exhausted. All of the young polecats were sold and this turned out to be my first ever business venture. I had managed to persuade the family that the female must breed to keep healthy. However, further breeding was to prove a step too far and I had to be content with just the one.

Like many teenagers, I started getting interested in rock music. The first record I bought was *Pretty Woman* by Roy Orbison. This was a fine place to start, but I quickly realised that there was much heavier music out there. One evening John surprised me by insisting that we watch *The Lulu Show.* I watched the programme and I was stunned. The Jimi Hendrix Experience appeared as special guests. They played the wildest music I'd ever heard and seemed supremely confident and relaxed. They were clearly having a ball. That was the beginning of my idea that rock musicians had more fun than anyone else on the planet. I bought the album Killer by Alice Cooper and that was the start of my real obsession with rock, as I began to realise that I may actually be

able to do this. Later I discovered Led Zeppelin and realised that the drums were the most exciting instrument in a rock band. I had tried most other instruments by then but as soon as I got to try a drum kit there was absolutely no doubt – this was the instrument for me. I started practising in the same obsessive manner that John had done with the timpani.

During my entire childhood my dad would be out nearly every weekend playing in a dance band. Whatever kids grow up with tends to become normal for them – for us it was natural for our dad to be playing music every weekend and that's pretty much what we all did when we grew up. We tended to have more money than most other families around us, partly because my dad had a well-paid job, and partly because of the extra income earned from his music. Several times various women would say to my mother, "How can you put up with him being out every Saturday night instead of taking you out?" She very wisely explained that she had a husband who was completely loyal and faithful, would never get drunk or gamble, was a fantastic father to her children and always kept the family comfortable. You don't have to look far to see husbands who don't have these qualities. She understood that for my dad, music was important and to stop him doing that would have made him miserable. The wives of other musicians would warn her that he might meet someone else and leave her. Again, she ignored them. Interestingly, most of their husbands did just that but my father didn't. Whenever there was music in the house, we would always badger my mum into singing and tease her that she sounded like Deanna Durbin, the singer and movie star of the 1930s and 40s.

One evening, after my dad had finished playing a gig with his dance band, I offered to give him a hand taking the equipment back to the car. He put a mike stand with a heavy base down on the pavement outside the hall and gave me strict instructions, "Stand there, don't move and keep an eye on this mike stand while I go and fetch the rest of the equipment." I said, "No problem" but felt slightly patronised that he had to say "Don't move!" A couple of friends of mine appeared and were chatting in the foyer of the venue. I just popped in there a few seconds to say hello but in view of my dad's instructions, ran straight back out to keep an eye on the mike stand. It

was gone! As we were on a corner I was able to quickly look up and down both streets and there was not a soul to be seen. I couldn't imagine any scenario where the mike stand could have been taken away so quickly. I thought if someone had roared up on a motorcycle, grabbed the mike stand and roared off, they could just about have got out of sight in time. Inevitably, my father appeared within a few seconds and said, "Where's the mike stand?" To which I replied, "It's gone!" My father said, "How could it have possibly gone if you were standing there?" I said, "I just popped in for a second." To which I got the inescapable, "I told you not to move from that spot!" Equipment in those days was way more expensive than it is now, but my father was never one to get upset about mere money — he knew he could always earn some more. Just about every musician in the world has gone through the agony of having his or her equipment stolen.

During my teen years my dad suffered quite badly from a bad back. He told me that pills never seemed to do him much good and he ended up going to see an osteopath, who made him better. I never went with him on any of those visits but I remember being intrigued that this guy could make him better whereas the pills could not. I actually looked into osteopathy but back in those days there was very little recognition and the course was not established as a university degree, which put me off. Of course, all of that has now changed.

In considering a career in medicine I started looking around for role models. There was a character on TV called Dr Kildare who was extremely good looking, had brilliant diagnostic skills and was always an object of admiration by all men and, more importantly, all women. I was very impressed with Dr Kildare but when I visited my local GP, Dr Chatterjee, I found the situation to be quite contrasting. Dr Chatterjee seemed to be inundated with extremely sick and elderly patients who kept moaning all the time. We had to sit in a waiting room with very thin walls and you could always hear everything that was being said in the consulting room. None of this bore any resemblance to the glamorous life of Dr Kildare.

One of the problems with attending a grammar school was that rugby was always the game of choice. I quickly learned the key to this game, which I will share with you: When you get the ball, throw it without pausing for a second. It doesn't really matter where you throw it. If you pause for a moment then ten other players will jump on you and it will hurt a lot. This is not the strategy used by the British Lions, but then they're not normal. Inexplicably, I didn't make the team. Those of us who weren't in the team were told to run around the field for 90 minutes. After an entire year of running around the field, the games teacher announced, "There is an opportunity for two boys to learn karate – who is interested?" I was very excited by this possibility but I paused to wonder whether I could ever do karate. During my three-second pause, two other boys raised their hands and were promptly selected. I spent the next two years running around a field for 90 minutes wondering why I didn't just raise my hand. In my adult life I have never been shy of stepping forward. Perhaps that is why.

John went on to study timpani at the Royal College of Music – a very prestigious establishment. He had only been there one year when he started getting offers to perform with various orchestras. He got the chance to play on TV to a live audience of 200 million people. This was the Last Night of the Proms, the most viewed classical music concert in the world. John's success suggested that my father might have had a point when he told us we could do anything we want. I decided that I would like to play to millions of people too, but I would do it with a rock band.

When I got into the 6th form at the age of 16 we were able to go in and out of the 6th form common room, which felt like a big promotion. The first thing that I did at that stage was to put a sign in the window saying, 'Terry Chimes Fan Club – Join Here'. At that point none of my fellow pupils had any inkling as to my musical leanings and I guess they just saw it as a harmless joke, which of course it was. But deep down there was something of Mr Chimes trying to break out.

This was about the time when one of my life's great tragedies occurred. For some years, girls had been walking about in miniskirts, which were getting

shorter and shorter. Then, just as I got to the age when I might have a chance to get somewhere near them, some idiot designed the maxiskirt – which reached right down to the ankles. I didn't get to see girls' legs again until the punk movement started. If I'd had my way, the inventor of the maxi would have been taken out and flogged!

When people say, "I am getting old" I often respond with, "Only the good die young". This is said ironically but I believe there may be some truth in it. When I was 17 I hung around with a gang of friends. Peter Lydon was about six months younger than me. He was the nicest guy you could ever wish to meet in your life, always positive, always smiling and never had a bad word to say about anyone else. Those of us who used to hang around with him probably took all this for granted – it was just the way Peter was. The rest of us more than made up for his lack of negativity by our bitching and moaning. When I was 17 we all got the sudden shocking news that he had died in a motorcycle accident. Everyone was a bit stunned for a time, but we all just got on with our lives. I have never forgotten Peter but was pleasantly surprised when I went to visit my old scoutmaster, Bill Everett, around the year 2000 – he had a picture of Peter on his wall. It was nice to see that Peter was not forgotten. In my practice I come across lots of families who have lost a young person and they always seem to be saying the same thing – that the one they lost was the nicest of the bunch. Maybe it's because they have died young that people say such things about them but I remain unconvinced by this as I have seen too many genuinely nice people leave this world very early in their lives.

Around that time I got sick. I was not ill enough to miss school but my experience gave me a valuable insight into what it's like to suffer illness and pain. It certainly didn't seem very valuable to me at the time. I will explain the illness in a later chapter. My fascination with health and disease kept growing and was noticed by all those around me.

When I was 17 I applied to both medical and dental schools because I couldn't decide which of the two professions would suit me better. On the one hand, medicine seemed to have greater prestige, with more variety of practice. On the other hand, doctors always seemed to be dealing with people

who were dying and worked ridiculously long hours. Dentists seemed to have a good, independent working life. In fact, I discovered that dentistry is one of the most stressful professions in the world, with frightening levels of divorce, heart attack and suicide. I was surprised by this and for a while I thought that really wouldn't apply to me because of my happy disposition but then I realised that some of those suicides had most probably started off as happy people before they joined the dental profession.

I found the interviews for college discouraging in that the people interviewing me, without exception, were very serious, miserable old men in grey suits (they were probably about 40). I never came out of an interview at medical school feeling uplifted or inspired in any way. I can remember thinking quite consciously about who is more to be admired, Dr Kildare or Jimi Hendrix? Of course the answer to that question would depend on whom you asked. Most young people would, of course, say Jimi Hendrix whereas my mother, without hesitation, would have said Dr Kildare. Such musings as these are part and parcel of the process of reaching a decision to follow a particular career path.

Whilst I was preparing for my A-level exams, I decided it wouldn't hurt to audition with a professional band. I answered an ad in the paper and travelled quite a long distance to meet them. I played for what seemed a long time but in the end they decided they were not going to take me on because I was so young. I was slightly disappointed but was also aware that it would have been impossible for me to join as I had all these exams coming up and I couldn't realistically go on tour. They had an upcoming TV spot on a programme called *New Faces – a Talent Show*. Sure enough a few months later I sat in my parent's lounge and watched them on TV – they didn't win but it felt good to have a connection between people you have met in real life and people on TV. It can sometimes seem as though these two worlds – the world of TV and the world you inhabit – cannot be traversed. This is perhaps the secret of success for shows such as the *X Factor*.

One of the upshots of my audition was the discovery that professional bands play a hell of a lot louder than I was used to. From that point on I would

practise the drums at three times the volume. When my dad asked me why I was playing so much louder, I replied, "That's what professional musicians do," and he never argued with me. Some time after that conversation I was in the lounge when someone else was playing drums in the practice room. Every time they hit the drum, the TV picture would flicker. I asked my mother what was going on and she told me nonchalantly that the TV always did that. I instantly felt rather guilty about the vast number of hours of practice that I had carried out which had ruined the rest of the family's viewing experience. Looking back, I think our neighbours were either saints or stone deaf. They were treated to the sound of me bashing on the drums, John playing the timpani and my dad's band rehearsing every week. Just to put the icing on the cake, my brother, Bryn, also started a band when he was about 16 (although, luckily for the neighbours, John had moved out by then).

During my last year at school, I decided that Led Zeppelin were the best band in the world, mainly because they had the best drummer – John Bonham. Bonham played with such power and authority that the whole band was elevated beyond anything else you could hear at that time. No other musician has exerted such a positive influence on me as Bonham and anybody who wants to play drums in a hard rock band should give Bonham a thorough listening to. Unfortunately, Bonham died very young (aged 32), something that rock drummers have a habit of doing.

I once went to a studio to do some recording with three other musicians. We simply said hello and asked a few questions before getting started. The engineer looked straight at me and said, "You're the drummer, aren't you?" To which I replied, "Yes, but how do you know?" He said, "I've been in this business a long time and I can just tell." That intrigued me and ever since that day I have played the game of guessing which one is which whenever I meet a band. I also try to guess what profession someone is in when I meet a patient for the first time. It is surprising how often you can get it right.

Just after my 18th birthday, I had taken and passed all of my exams and finally had to make a decision about my future career. Unfortunately, there was just no profession that involved touring the world playing drums whilst

healing sick people. It seemed a choice had to be made. I think that one of the main factors in the decision-making process was that I could do music while I was young and change professions later. This idea sounded far more feasible than going to University and then becoming a musician afterwards. By this time I had been interviewed at medical schools and met lots of students and doctors. The impression I had was that if you followed that path you would have extremely limited time for yourself and certainly not nearly enough time to play in a band.

And so Mr Chimes won the argument and I decided to join a band. It would be some time before I started to earn any money playing music so I needed to work. I took a job in the school laboratory. There were several advantages to this; my science qualifications allowed me to earn a reasonable salary, I knew all the people there and got on with them and most importantly it was easy to get time off to play music. Furthermore, I managed to save enough money to rent a flat and buy a car.

I decided that to hit the big time I needed to keep auditioning until I found the right band. I would scour the pages of *Melody Maker* (the now defunct magazine which everybody then used to find musicians) and audition for any band that sounded like it was half decent. The process was as follows: I would carry all my drums from my upstairs flat into my car downstairs, drive to the place of audition, bring my drums into the place, unpack them, set them up, play for a few minutes, pack up the drums, carry them to the car, drive home, carry the drums upstairs from the car and that was that.

It seemed like 90 percent of the people I was auditioning for were either useless or just didn't seem as if they were going anywhere! Yet I pushed on week after week after week because I had a profound belief that I would, at some point, find the right band. If you asked me where this belief came from, I'd say it was a combination of my dad telling me I could do anything, the band I auditioned with appearing on TV and then seeing my brother on TV playing to millions of people. All of these things had happened in my life and the obvious next step was me being on TV playing to millions of people.

No amount of cynicism or derision would dampen my belief. After endless months of searching, my patience was soon to be rewarded.

CHAPTER 2
THE CLASH PART I (1976-1977)

"People who say it cannot be done should not interrupt those who are doing it."

George Bernard Shaw

I phoned in response to an ad for a drummer and spoke to a very peculiar man. I didn't like the sound of him but he had a sort of confidence that intrigued me. We arranged an audition but I had to meet him in a café first, which seemed a bit odd. The café was called Ortin's Kitchen in Praed Street, Paddington. I met a diminutive thirty-something man with glasses who seemed to make a point of not being friendly. I had to ask him his name, which was Bernard. At the time I thought this was about the most uncool name you could have. He then proceeded to ask me some strange questions such as, "What do you think is going on right now?" To which I replied, "What is going on right now is that I am sitting in a café with you instead of auditioning with a band!" I quickly discovered that whether you were rude or polite to this man made no difference. There was something, however, that I liked about him. He was really serious about what he was doing. This was in stark contrast to the many people I had auditioned with who seemed to think that success was simply a matter of luck. Bernard was quite certain that luck had nothing to do with anything, which interested me. After talking for half an hour or so, it seemed I was worthy of going on to the next step, which was auditioning with the other musicians.

We walked around the corner to a basement studio. There were various people down there, three musicians with whom I was going to play and a few others who sort of reminded me of people you might see at a party in a

1960's movie. Most of them were decidedly odd but I reasoned that was to be expected in this game. I was relieved when I met the bass player because he seemed friendly, bright and articulate and understood my desire to get on and play the music rather than talk nonsense. The bass player was Tony James, whom I was later to join in Generation X with Billy Idol. He would also go on to mastermind the pop phenomenon that was Sigue Sigue Sputnik. There was a guitarist who was quieter and more focused on his guitar. This was Brian James who would later form The Damned. There was also Mick who played guitar and did a bit of singing. At this stage I really didn't know what to make of Mick although when we got to play I realised that it was really the music he was here for. I actually can't remember what happened after the audition. I felt that it was an interesting experience but the band certainly wasn't ready to go and perform, it was more of an embryonic work in progress.

I carried on auditioning with various people and eventually answered another ad. I told Bernard I recognised his voice and he replied that he remembered me too because I reminded him of a young doctor. I said, "What do you mean?" He replied, "I can just imagine you saying, 'here are your pills, madam!' At that stage Bernard knew nothing of my medical leanings and I must grudgingly credit him with impressive insight. He invited me to come down to a new location in Hammersmith. He told me that Mick had 'graduated' from the training of the previous band but the others hadn't.

I got there to find someone called Wally (full name Warwick Nightingale) whom I later discovered was the original guitarist with the Sex Pistols. Wally was the key-holder for this rehearsal place. He was very friendly and pleasant and told me that the others would be here soon. He'd had to rush off unexpectedly to buy some alcohol for his father whom he informed me was an alcoholic. This was obviously a normal thing for him to do but I remember being struck at that moment by how lucky I had been because, in my world, parents did things for you – not the other way round.

The rest of the band arrived. There was a bass player called Paul who basically didn't seem to speak, and Mick, whom I remembered from before. There was a singer called Billy (Watts) and a guitarist called Keith Levine, who

was even more stroppy than Bernard. As I walked with them from the café back to the studio, it struck me that everyone had the same look – unusual clothes (drainpipes not flares, bright shirts – some with painting on them) and very short hair. Passers by were staring at them. They had the appearance of a gang of like-minded people. I think all young men have a primal instinct to join a gang and of course a band is the best kind of gang because you don't get beaten up so much!

I enjoyed the audition more than the previous one because there seemed to be a stronger direction and a clearer vision of how we were trying to sound. Billy was interesting because he put an awful lot of energy into being the front man and made some weird-looking faces. A few weeks later I talked to Bernard again and he invited me to yet another venue – this time in Camden Town. I came down expecting to see the same faces and I was rather shocked that Billy had been replaced by someone called Joe – apparently the new singer. It may sound silly but I felt a sort of loyalty to Billy and a sadness that he had disappeared. When I met Joe, I was unsure whether he was an improvement or not. He didn't look anything like a rock singer, he didn't dress like anyone in a band and his speaking voice was very croaky and strange. I found it difficult to see him as a front man in a rock band, especially compared to Billy. However, I realised there must be something about this guy or they wouldn't have replaced Billy with him, so I determined to wait and see.

When we started playing, the band sounded better – there were fewer cover songs and a much harder edge to the music. This matched nicely with my John Bonham style heavy-handed drumming. I came to realise that Joe Strummer was the best possible front man for this band – but that was a gradual realisation not a sudden light bulb moment. Joe was a very warm-hearted, sensitive person who really cared about those who were around him. This made it easy to like him, even though he could drive you crazy at times. In addition, Mick was always happy to lighten the mood with humour and Paul actually started speaking, although not very much. I suppose you could say that The Clash was formed that day.

The band worked like crazy seven days a week. Bernard had masterminded the whole project and he created a hothouse in which everybody was expected to perform 110% and to work on every level – the music, the stage set, the clothes we wore and the attitudes we expressed. It was a strange period because we were constantly under pressure, even though that pressure was self-inflicted. That stage seemed to go on and on but I know from reading various books about The Clash that, while it felt like years, it couldn't have been for more than a few months. We were sitting in a pub one night and Keith rather unexpectedly said, "Do you really want to be in this band?" and I said "Yes, of course!" So he said, "OK then, you're in!" He called over to Bernard and said I was now officially the drummer. This irritated Bernard who said, "I make those decisions, not anyone else." This exasperated me and I said to the pair of them "Of course I'm the drummer – who else is going to be?" and no more was said.

At that time, we were desperate to play to a live audience. Bernard kept on telling us that we weren't quite ready but he never said when we would be, nor gave us any kind of criteria by which to judge when the time had come. Meanwhile, we decorated the rehearsal space in Camden Town that was called 'Rehearsals, Rehearsals' – I can't remember who thought of that name but it was very appropriate. Paul painted a huge urban landscape on the wall behind the stage. Painting for Paul was like medicine for me. Paul had decided that the life of an artist was a bit lonely when you were 20 years old and that it would be better to be in a band first. In a strangely parallel way I had decided that people don't like an old musician because they are out of date and no one likes a young doctor, as they are not old enough to know anything.

After what seemed like an eternity in the hothouse (even though it was cold and damp) we got to play our first gig at a pub in Sheffield: The Black Swan, or The Mucky Duck, as we used to call it. We were to support the Sex Pistols. Our enthusiasm levels were so high for that first show that I got up at four in the morning to be at the rehearsal place by five to leave for Sheffield, about 200 miles away. We were playing at around 7pm. This may seem ridiculous now, but the fact that we left so early was a sign of our enthusiasm and eagerness to get there and do a great job.

I knew about the Sex Pistols but had never heard them play. The first member I met was Glen Matlock, the bass player. He was very friendly and said he was looking forward to hearing us play. Then I met Johnny Rotten who was ranting and raving about his dislike of dogs and his preference for cats. He seemed weird enough to be the front man in a rock band. Paul Cook the drummer and Steve Jones the guitarist both seemed very quiet. After the sound check I met Malcolm McLaren, the man who created the punk movement. They say that first impressions make an impact. My first impression of Malcolm was that he was wearing a T-shirt upon which was painted a pair of large naked female breasts. That's not particularly unusual these days but it was unheard of then. Nevertheless, he was very helpful to us on our first gig. I told Paul Simonon that I thought Malcolm was a bit weird – he burst into laughter and said, "He's okay when you get used to him!"

After we finished our gig and packed up, Joe and I spent the next hour watching The Pistols play. He liked the band a lot and was keen to see what I made of them. They played a very tight set and were clearly a battle-hardened touring band with lots of experience. However, what impressed Joe and myself the most was John Lydon's charisma and humour. After that gig the thought occurred to me that this band, The Sex Pistols, were at the same time our comrades in arms and our competition.

Next up Bernie booked a show at 'Rehearsal, Rehearsals' for people in the music business on Friday August 13th. Such a performance is often referred to as a 'Showcase'. Of course Bernard would do the inviting and none of us had any idea who was going to come. Everybody was happy to leave these things to Bernard as he seemed to have a flair for it. He invited some journalists – but not many, so that the ones who were invited felt special. This ploy seemed to work because we instantly got the press on our side. Because we had been in a hot-house for so long the pressure was unbearable. I remember Mick throwing up several times before the performance whereas Joe was quite relaxed about it. After the performance, Mick was fine and Joe was depressed. This response pattern was exactly the same many years later when I toured the States with the band. Because of the pressure, there was a

feeling that when we finally played we unleashed all that pent-up energy on the audience. It almost felt like we were doing violence to them – although most clearly liked it!

NEAR DEATH EXPERIENCE NUMBER I

The Clash played a gig and got back to the rehearsal studio quite late to find all the cars locked in by a bolted gate. Having no way to get home until morning we settled down to sleep in the rehearsal studio. It was unbelievably cold that night so we assembled every conceivable form of heating and turned them on. One device was an electric single ring cooker, which you could use to boil a pot on. We then laid down on chairs or sofas or whatever we could find, grabbing whatever cushions were around. I was woken a couple of hours later by Micky Foote, our sound engineer. As I opened my eyes, I could only see a couple of feet in front of my face as the room was filled with thick, black smoke. Everyone was coughing uncontrollably as we had all breathed thick fumes for some time before waking up. We opened all the windows, as freezing was preferable to being killed by the fumes. I have wondered since then about how easily it could have been the end of us that night – had Micky not woken up. Perhaps the current obsession with fire retardant materials and smoke alarms is not such a bad idea.

———•—•———

Having survived that experience, we next played the Roundhouse in Camden Town. Here Joe made one of his speeches during which he said, "We haven't got O and A levels and all that." (The qualifications required for university entrance in the UK). Someone in the front row shouted, "Your drummer has!" Joe later confessed to me that he couldn't think of an answer to that so he just went into the next song.

When I came to rehearsals one day, Mick and Joe were discussing Keith. Joe had expressed the idea that Keith was a phantom guitarist who came in and played and left. Joe felt that Keith wasn't really a part of what we were doing. Mick replied that he understood what Joe meant and said, "Do you think he should leave then?" Joe agreed and, to my astonishment, so did Paul. I was shocked because this appeared to be such a sudden and random decision. I now think they were right because they had been thinking about it for a long time and then discovered that they'd all been feeling the same way. When Keith arrived soon after we gave him the news, which he took quite well, although he wasn't happy about it. At that moment there was the feeling that we then had to turn our attention to what we would sound like as a 4-piece. Mick summed it up by saying, "I'd better learn how to play the guitar!" He could of course already play the guitar but up until that point it was Keith's job to do any solos, whereas now it would be up to Mick. Although we were now a 4-piece band we still needed a lot of other people to help us.

Micky Foote had worked with Joe previously. He was a loyal, hardworking, uncomplaining person who naturally stepped into the role of being our sound engineer. Another character was Sebastian Conran. When we met him he was studying design. He just walked up to us, having enjoyed the gig, and asked if we would like a hand carrying the gear out. No band ever says no to this kind of offer. From that point on he just sort of joined the team. Apparently he had previously booked the Sex Pistols to play at the Central School of Art and Design, where he had been studying. Sebastian is a very cheerful and positive person, which makes him good to have around. We later realised that his dad was the famous Terence Conran, the designer and store-owner. There was something comically ironic about having the son of a rich and famous person helping a Punk band, whose members all came from poor backgrounds. Talking of design, we needed a lot of new clothes. The right designs were hard to find as they had to be different. Bernard drafted in Alex Michon – a confirmed fashion fanatic who worked upstairs at 'Rehearsals', which manufactured a continuous supply of jackets and trousers.

Sebastian was also a motorbike fanatic – he took me for a ride on his bike once. I was not used to bikes so every time he leaned the bike to the left I would lean the other way to try and straighten it up which made the bike wobble all over the place. It was probably Sebastian's influence that started my love affair with motorbikes. I rode several motorbikes but after about three years I decided to stop, as riding bikes and a long life seemed to be mutually exclusive. This was later to be repeatedly confirmed in my second career – I've lost count of the motorcycle accident victims I've seen.

One day Sebastian talked Joe into riding from London to a venue in Manchester on the back of his bike. Joe was able to leave later than us as bikes are faster and he arrived just after us. The problem was that the temperature was below zero. I'll never forget the sight of Joe walking in – he looked like Quasimodo. He was so frozen that he couldn't even speak! We all burst into laughter, having heard from Joe earlier that he was going to be so much cooler than us arriving on a motorbike. Sebastian was still around when I left The Clash but seemed to have moved on by the time I re-joined the band in 1982, five years later.

Sebastian had a brother called Jasper who was a budding dress designer. He seemed to be as passionate about dress design as we were about music. They had a large house in Regent's Park that we often used to go to. We all turned up there one night, drunk as lords. We staggered through the corridor and tripped on an extension cable that crossed the hall. This cable was being used by Jasper to power his sewing machine. He was burning the midnight oil, working late on his latest creation. He emerged from the room in a rage. Obviously the power had gone off as we tripped on the wire and apparently ruined whatever he was doing at that moment. As he stood there, screaming hysterically at us all, we weren't sure whether to commiserate, apologise or laugh. It's difficult to convince a bunch of drunken rock musicians of the vital importance of the last seam that was not properly sewn. I dare say that Sebastian managed to placate him later. I think of that moment whenever I see some of Jasper's clothes in a store!

Bernard started looking after some other bands, notably the Subway Sect. Vic Goddard was the main man in that band and was a gifted songwriter whom Bernard always had a lot of faith in – sometimes to the annoyance of Mick Jones. The Baker was their roadie and was later to work for many years with the Clash. He was a short, stocky guy with a baby-face and a shaved head. His dry, cynical sense of humour seemed to help him survive the crazy world he had come to inhabit. He was hard-working and reliable, which is what we really needed.

During those early gigs you could never predict what was going to happen. We played a punk festival at the 100 Club, a long-established venue at No. 100 Oxford Street. There was some fighting in the audience that I didn't take much notice of. It was in the heat wave summer of 1976 and being a packed house it got really hot. After we'd played I decided to get some fresh air. I walked out the front door and before I knew it, two guys I had never seen before kicked me in the face. Apparently they had been thrown out earlier for fighting and were going to attack the very next person who came out of the door, who happened to be me! After the kick in the face, I did karate training for a number of years, although I was never particularly good at it. There have been two subsequent attempts to punch or kick me, both of which I fortunately managed to foil and get out of without any harm being done.

Another time we played a gig in a basement in Guildford. During this show the audience started to reduce in number until there were only a few people left. That was definitely not what normally happened. We finished our set and sat there somewhat bewildered. The manager of the club came over and explained that there had been a battle in the bar upstairs between the punks and the off-duty soldiers (there is a garrison in the town) and then hundreds of policemen arrived to make it a 3-way war. When we came upstairs the place was totally empty and absolutely wrecked.

During 1976 there were punks springing up all over the place and at the same time there was a Teddy Boy revival. Unfortunately, we started hearing about clashes (no pun intended) between Punks and Teddy Boys – somewhat similar to the battles between Mods and Rockers in the sixties. We were

booked to play at the University of London Union, on a bill that featured several Punk and Teddy Boy Bands, It seems that some genius thought that by putting us on the same bill we would somehow come together – a bit like locking cats and dogs in a garden shed together! I had not realised this until it was too late because this gig, bizarrely, was the only Clash gig that my parents came along to. They were naturally curious to find out what their son had been doing 24hours a day seven days a week for the past six months.

During the sound check a little skinny guy came up to us and asked the band, the crew and various other individuals if we wouldn't mind helping him lift a full-size concert grand piano onto the stage. Shakin' Stevens was on the bill and would need it. We felt sorry for him so we did it but I remember remarking to Joe, "I hope I don't have to lift one of those ever again!" The first band on the bill was called Please Yourself. Joe Strummer's comment was that they might as well have called themselves 'Why Bother?' They played their entire set to an audience consisting of Micky Foot's dog, Gertie, and my parents! By the time we came on there was a lot of fighting between Punks and Teds in the audience. Our set seemed to pour petrol on the fire and at one stage Paul Simonon had to take a swing at some of the Teds with his Fender base. Fortunately, we all got out in one piece. As this was an afternoon rather than an evening show, I popped over to my parents to see what they had thought of it. They had clearly discussed the matter and decided not to say anything about the violence. When I came in my dad said something about how nice and tight the beginnings and endings of the songs were. My mum said very little. I tried to explain to them that large-scale punch-ups were not a feature of every show we did but I'm not sure they were convinced.

The Clash played The Institute of Contemporary Art in 1976. There was a couple sitting right at the front. The man was very drunk and the girl seemed to be biting him on the ear, although I wasn't sure. Then his ear started bleeding profusely. She then picked up a broken bottle and looked like she wasn't sure whether to slice his ear off completely or start to carve up her own body. This is very distracting when you are trying to play a gig, as I, for one, felt he needed rescuing. Eventually the security people removed them

both, much to our relief. This reinforced my view that you have to be very careful when choosing a girlfriend or a wife. Years later I discovered that the young man had been Shane MacGowan from the band, The Pogues.

On another occasion, we had a Spanish photographer called Rocco Macauly taking photographs and, without any warning, the American singer Patti Smith jumped on the stage and started dancing like crazy. Instead of photographing this one-off event, Rocco failed to recognise her and pulled her off the stage, thinking she was a random nutcase. This was such a shame as he had worked so hard and then missed his big chance. After the show Bernie took great pleasure in berating Rocco in front of everyone.

Bernie surprised everybody one day by announcing that he'd bought a car with the number plate CLA5H. He said that he wasn't really interested in that sort of thing but that Micky would like it. In fact, Micky was the last man on earth to get excited by a personalised number plate and immediately said so. I have no idea who ended up with the number plate. A side of the Clash that nobody has ever seen manifested itself in a phase when we would drive from one place to another singing ludicrous songs. I think it started by us singing arrangements of the songs that we were performing so that we would remember them accurately but inevitably it became ridiculous, the silliest songs we sang being a Swingle number and 'Terry' by Twinkle where the lyrics said, "He rode into the night in his Triumph Herald" (the car I was driving at the time).

Another memorable character from that period was Sid Vicious. He was always hanging around the studio. He seemed to be searching for some part to play in this whole Punk movement. He was a strong character with a continual flow of new ideas. He would often turn up in all sorts of different clothes. I got the impression he saw us as a group of people to whom he could take his ideas without fear of ridicule. He started off playing drums with a band called The Flowers of Romance who supported us at one of our gigs. He later switched to bass guitar. I regarded him then as a friendly, engaging person although he liked to challenge everybody's opinions.

He turned up once at the studio and told me he hadn't eaten for two days. He looked sort of grey so I took him to the café and bought him a fry-up. I was glad to do this for him as he looked like he was about to die. But I did wonder at the time where his next meal was coming from. During the time I knew him there was a steady continual change from the friendly pleasant 18-year-old that I had first met, to someone who was more and more interested in violence. I remember seeing him at a gig we were playing, at the Royal College of Art, punching someone in the audience. I asked some of the guys in the band what was going on but no one seemed to know why he was changing and what was happening to him.

While we were recording the first Clash album we got the news that The Pistols had parted company with Glenn Matlock and bought in Sid on bass. The four of us reflected that the Pistols now had a very strong front line and that's when the discussion about The Pistols being allies or competitors came up. I can remember voicing this idea to the other guys in the band during the making of our first album. Joe instantly agreed with me that they were the band for us to beat whereas Mick was strongly of the opinion that they were our allies and we should never think of them as our competition. I suppose with the benefit of hindsight we could say that Mick was right on this one.

It must have been about two years later that I heard that Sid was in prison accused of murdering his girlfriend Nancy. The Clash actually played a benefit gig to help him. He took his own life whilst awaiting trial. As soon as I heard that news I remembered Sid saying to the press during 1976, "I'll die before I'm 25, and when I do I'll have lived the way I wanted to." At the time, I regarded that statement as nonsense. Sid's death seemed like a tremendous waste to me. Talking of death, I remember remarking to the guys in The Clash that the best thing would be for one of us to die, because then you automatically become a legend! I was of course talking with tongue-in-cheek, not thinking for one moment that it would actually happen. The Clash were not particularly into drugs at that time, and we probably couldn't have afforded them anyway. Mick and Joe would occasionally smoke joints but that

was about it. I was always more interested in beer, which put me into a party mood, rather than dope, which put me to sleep.

Eventually, we started getting interest from record companies. As usual, we let Bernard do all the negotiating on that front. At the time it seemed like a good idea. I later changed my mind about that but now, with hindsight, I'm back to thinking it was a good idea! Bernard was able to drive a hard bargain, which he would have been unable to do if there were four other people negotiating and commenting. A Kiwi called Chris Parry was the one I remember most clearly, perhaps because he was a fellow drummer. As head of A&R for Polydor Records, he was very keen and actually put us in a studio to do some demos.

The demos were to be produced by the legendry Guy Stevens. Guy had worked with numerous bands including 'Free' and 'Mott the Hoople', so he automatically had the absolute trust of the band. Although an alcoholic at the time, he was an incredible character. I immediately warmed to him, partly because of his illustrious past and partly because he was such a charismatic man. I can still see him jumping up and down in front of Mick while he played his guitar parts. I found it hilarious because I used to always think of producers as the cool ones sitting in a chair taking control.

A situation arose when the studio people and the record company weren't happy with Guy, whom they regarded as an alcohol-soaked has-been. Guy cracked under the pressure and screwed up the mix. With hindsight, if we had been more experienced the band could have given him the necessary confidence and security and it would have worked. As it turned out, Guy was out of the picture for the time being. Joe in particular felt sad that it hadn't worked out with Guy. His comment to me was, "They've got him numbered." Guy did come back later, however, to produce the Clash album, 'London Calling.' Guy died at the age of 38 from prescription drugs he was taking to reduce his alcohol dependency.

Just weeks after we completed the demos, the news broke that we were to sign to CBS not Polydor and the whole thing was done in a flash.

The whole story of me quitting the band has never been told. This is because I had decided to leave for private reasons that I didn't want to discuss with the press. Having little experience with the press, I didn't know that what they do in situations when they don't know the facts, is simply to make them up. One paper printed a story that I left because somebody threw a bottle at me during one of the shows. That would have been ridiculous, as hundreds of things had been thrown at the stage at one time or another and nobody really worried about that. That story has been repeated endlessly because it is the only story out there. If nothing else, the music business taught me never to believe what you read in the papers. The real reason why I left was a very simple one – I wasn't enjoying it! I had made a promise to myself that I would never do a job I didn't enjoy and I intended to keep this promise. I was constantly arguing with everybody else. It tended to be me on one side, with the band, management and anyone else who happened to be there, on the other side. It was only years later that I understood the real reason for this.

Politics was often said to be the main subject of all the arguments, but that's not actually the way it was. A full understanding of what was really going on didn't come to me until thirty years later – when I learned a lot more about human nature by treating thousands of patients. I can now see very clearly why there seemed to be a difference in attitude between myself and everybody else. I came from a very happy family and grew up full of optimism, always smiling (except in rock band photos – you never smile in those in case you end up looking like ABBA). In stark contrast, everybody else seemed to come from a broken home. All I ever heard from them, including the road crew and management, was how terrible the world was and how it was going to get much worse. Bernie saw this as training for our mission and actively encouraged this constant diatribe against the world. Baker referred to it as the 'Stalinist regime'.

During the various arguments we had in the early days, they would say something like, "We don't want to earn any money, we'll just give it away." My answer would be, "So, what are you going to eat?" And also, "I don't want to give my money away, I want to buy a sports car." I liked fast cars but never wanted a Lamborghini, although I have read hundreds of times in the press and in books that I did.

After a great deal of soul-searching I turned up at rehearsals one day and told the others that I wanted to leave. When I made my announcement I think they were genuinely shocked as we had worked very hard to get where we were. The shock turned to anger and then came: "We'll just find someone else then". I had agreed to carry on doing the shows until they found someone so as not to impede the progress of the band. They auditioned a very large number of other drummers but they were unable to find one who fitted the bill. Then they seemed to feel that it would be easier to persuade me to stay rather than find an adequate replacement. At that point Bernard the manager tried very hard to change my mind. This was difficult for him, as he simply didn't understand my reasons for leaving.

He even telephoned my father in an effort to persuade me to stay. The idea of Bernard trying to convince my dad is hilarious to me. I wish I had a recording of that conversation. Of one thing I'm sure – for the first time in his life, Bernard would have done more listening than talking.

He told me that he saw my role as being a foil for the others. In other words, the challenges and arguments that I was coming up with would prepare the other guys for when they stepped out of the safety of the rehearsal room and were challenged by the press. I told him that it might be a useful role but not one that I enjoyed.

The failure to find a suitable replacement despite auditioning an endless series of drummers (over 200) prompted me to say to the Baker that it must have been soul-destroying for them. He replied, "I picked them all up, helped set up their kits and took them home – so don't tell me it was soul-destroying for the band!" Accordingly, I didn't sign any contract at that time but I did

agree to record the single that was to be 'White Riot'. Recording the single seemed to go by in a flash. We had Micky Foote producing, even though he wasn't really a producer. However the idea was to capture the sound and energy of the live shows at that time so production wasn't really a priority. We needed to create some chaos on that record so we found an alarm bell and had several people jumping up and down on a wooden board. First to volunteer for this job was Sebastian, who seemed to enjoy that experience more than anyone else. I can remember the odd feeling of being in a club and hearing your own record played for the first time. It's quite special, like the feeling of hearing yourself on the radio for the first time.

Next came the job of recording the first album. They still hadn't found a drummer so I agreed to do it and I was pleased about this because it felt like I had done an awful lot of work to help get the band to that point and here was a chance to put it down on record forever.

When you record an album the first job is to get the sound of each instrument right before you start playing any songs. We spent a couple of hours doing that with the drums, maybe 20 minutes with the guitar but when we came to the bass there was a problem. Paul was a major reggae fan and had a very clear idea how he wanted the bass to sound: very bassy. Mick had other ideas. He felt that we needed to hear the notes clearly and wanted a completely different sound. The argument between the two of them went on for hours and hours with neither one giving an inch. I was aware that the cost of a studio like this was something like £200 or £300 an hour – over 100 times the minimum wage (although there was no minimum wage then). After about 4 hours, I was beginning to lose the will to live, and so was Joe. I would often be the one to try and make peace between people but in this case I had no idea where to start. Then the engineer saved the day with a piece of diplomatic genius. He suggested that we record both sounds simultaneously on different tracks and argue about it later. Joe and I nearly banged into each other in our haste to agree with the new idea. Once that obstacle was out of the way the recording went at a cracking pace. Since 90% of the time we were simply reproducing what we were doing live, and as we had played those songs at loads of gigs by this time, we could do it with our eyes shut.

The exception to this was 'Police and Thieves', which we never performed live in those days. This song was something we used to play for fun because it made a change from the other stuff. We would play it during a sound check whilst people were adjusting levels to get the sound right. I can't recall at what stage it went from being a bit of fun in a sound check to a track in the album, but I do remember being amazed when I heard the mixed version. Mick had added some very rhythmic guitar chords and very high vocal harmonies. These two changes completely transformed the song into many people's favourite track on the album. It was an early indication of Mick's talent as a studio animal. Personally, I always preferred live performances to studio recording because you could feed off the energy of the audience – like a vampire sucking blood.

During the time that I was leaving, Joe came to terms with my love of sports cars and told me that my desire for an E-type Jag was essentially no different from his desire for a Volkswagen Camper Van. He actually offered me his initial share of the record company advance to buy a sports car in an effort to persuade me to stay in the band. Obviously I would never have taken it, and my reasons for leaving were nothing to do with cars or money. He was just trying to find a compromise and he had come to realise that having the right person in the band was more important than what type of car they drove.

I remember being with Joe in The Roxy, a punk nightclub. Don Letts was the DJ there and would later make videos for The Clash and many other bands. We bumped into an American called Lee Childers who was the manager of various bands including 'Johnny Thunders'. Lee said something about always being on the look-out for a good drummer and Joe surprised me by saying that if I went to play for one of Lee's bands he would kill both of us and finished that with, "That's fair, isn't it?" Of course Joe would never kill anybody but I was surprised at that stage by the strength of his feelings. Lots of people tried either to persuade me to stay or at least to figure out why I was going. Sebastian, Micky Foote and Sid Vicious all tried, but the philosophy of, "Do what you love" didn't seem to mean anything to any of them. Especially when large sums of money were heading our way.

Sometime after the first album was finished, the day finally arrived when The Clash found a new drummer, Nick Headon, soon to be known as Topper. Bernard announced this to me, saying, "You must be very upset?" which I found strange because I had been trying to leave for nearly a year. They asked me if I minded meeting Topper to go through a few drum things, which I was happy to do. We went down to the Camden café, always a favourite haunt, just by Camden Lock. We got on extremely well and exchanged all the necessary information whilst we had lunch. When we had finished eating, I realised I had forgotten my wallet, which is always bad when meeting someone for the first time, but he was fine about it. We didn't meet again for about five years.

The day came when I played what I thought would be my last ever gig with The Clash, at Lanchester Polytechnic in Coventry. Paul even sprayed the word Goodbye onto my t-shirt especially for the occasion. After that show I gave that t-shirt to my nephew Joe (Bryn's step-son). He recently gave it back to me mounted in a big picture frame with all sorts of memorabilia from that time which was a wonderful surprise. I decided early on not to keep memorabilia and so it was particularly good to have such a souvenir. Joe is now a seriously good DJ and has played at many of my parties, although he chooses to do that where he now lives, in the Far East. I don't think Joe Strummer ever forgave me for quitting, but more of that later.

The Clash was my first proper band and had become very popular very quickly. I'd been a teenager when I joined and, like many teenagers, had a ludicrous level of over-confidence. I thought I would simply go out and do it again. I had a shock coming — it wasn't going to be that easy.

CHAPTER 3
GENERATION X

"A champion is afraid of losing. Everyone else is afraid of winning."

Billie Jean King

Shortly after leaving The Clash in 1977, I bumped into Bernard Rhodes who suggested that I go out on tour with a French all-girl band. This was not to play, but to give them a bit of help and advice. Since I was only 20 at the time it seemed like an odd idea. I asked him where they were touring and he said Italy, to which I immediately replied, "I'm in!" We toured Italy, which was a very strange place musically at the time. It seemed like Punk had arrived but no one knew what it was supposed to sound or look like. I don't know how much help I was to the band but I certainly managed to sample a great deal of Italian food and wine. After one particularly heavy night I spent most of the day in bed. The chef at the small hotel where we were staying actually came into my room in the evening and said in broken English, "You have to eat or you will die!" It was a fun trip but on my return I realised I would have to get back to playing in a band.

I had heard all about Johnny Thunders and The Heartbreakers from Joe Strummer and Mick Jones who had just worked with them on 'The Anarchy in the UK' Tour. Actually, most of the shows on that tour were cancelled because of the Sex Pistols infamous swearing on live TV. Thunders was well ahead of his time – he was only two years older than me and yet when I joined The Clash at the age of 19 he was already known worldwide as a guitarist with The New York Dolls. The New York Dolls was one of the bands that had two drummers die before anyone else in the band. Mick and Joe at that time were raving about the Heartbreaker's drummer, the late Jerry Nolan. I

asked Joe why he hadn't asked Jerry to join The Clash and he sort of frowned and said something about him being from a different culture (I don't know if he meant being American or the drug culture that Jerry was fond of) and also being 30 years old. It seems hilarious now to think that 30 felt extremely old to us at that time. Some months later I got a call asking me to come along and see The Heartbreakers with a view to joining them. It seems there was some problem with Jerry but I can't remember what it was. I was quite excited to see them, after what Mick and Joe had said, and was not disappointed. The band played a great set of brilliant songs, had lots of energy and the audience loved them. I subsequently went down to rehearse with them and we all got on very well.

Before I knew it, we were off on tour together. The first gig I played was in Amsterdam. This was one of the first Punk shows to be held in Amsterdam. I will never forget that when we left the stage at the end of our set, which was about 45 minutes, it seemed that every single member of the audience simultaneously looked at their watches. They had apparently been used to listening to hippy bands who went on and on for hours. The promoters asked us to go back and do some more. I pointed out that my hands were already bleeding, as I had given all that I had (I hadn't yet discovered the wonders of golf gloves!).

We went to a nightclub after the show and the owner of the club said, "If you get up and play one song, I will give you free champagne all night." I think we were already drunk anyway but we took him up on his offer. I don't remember anything else about this (I was as drunk as a skunk) but my friends told me that when the resident band came back to take over, I told the drummer to get lost as I was playing now and actually played the rest of the set. It is very scary when you have done something like that and can't remember one single minute.

These guys were very different from The Clash, and not the slightest bit interested in politics. They were more interested in wine, women and song, although not necessarily in that order.

When I tell people that I spent fifteen years touring with rock bands, they often snigger and ask, "What about all those girls then, eh?" There's a widespread belief that rock musicians spend 5% of their time playing music, 45% sleeping and 50% having sex. It's true that when you are touring with a rock band, girls tend to throw themselves at you. There's a downside to this. The ones whom you would like to throw themselves at you usually don't. Worse than that, the ones you would really rather not throw themselves at you usually do. Most guys in bands have had much more than their fair share of casual sex. In the seventies it was strangely un-cool to use condoms. This may sound odd to younger people but before AIDS came along, there was much less pressure to use protection as so many girls were on the pill. I remember telling some fellow band members that I'd never had a sexually transmitted disease. They were amazed, having had such problems multiple times. I concluded fairly early in the game that unwanted pregnancies or diseases would really spoil my plans, even though I didn't have any plans!

I did once seduce a very attractive girl and whisk her off to my hotel room for the night. Later, after we had both calmed down, she pronounced that "Drummers are better lovers." I enquired as to the origins of this idea and her reply was a long list of well-known drummers that she had bedded. As this list was trotted out I reached two conclusions: Firstly, I decided that, knowing some of these guys, it was probably all true. Secondly, I realised that I'd just joined the list. This and other experiences led me to the conclusion that there is a lot to be said for monogamous relationships. It was something I was to get involved in within a couple of years.

On my 21st birthday, I went shopping with my mother and she bought me the finest leather jacket I had ever seen. I loved that jacket and wore it all the time. One Saturday night I was playing pool in a pub in Hemel Hempstead. I took my jacket off to improve my pool playing technique. At the end of the

evening, when I went to pick up my jacket to go home, it had disappeared. Now there was no way I was going to put up with it disappearing. I searched all over for it but it had definitely left the building. It was now quite late and not many people were left in the pub. Those I asked had no recollection of seeing anybody take it. I was with my friend George, who lived in Hemel Hempstead, which is about 40 miles from London, where I lived. I told George as we left that I would get that jacket back, whatever it takes.

I was not just focused on that goal, I was obsessed with it and no power in the universe was going to stop me. George, however, didn't have any emotional attachment to the jacket, and so he focused on the obstacles: First, we had no idea who took it. Second, we had no way of finding out. And third, I lived 40 miles away. When you focus very hard on the outcome, the obstacles somehow become much smaller. At that time, to me, the obstacles he described were tiny molehills, whereas he saw them as mountains.

The following evening I made the trip back to Hemel Hempstead, and took the long-suffering George with me back to the pub. I asked every person in the pub whether they were there the previous evening, if they had seen anything, and did they know anybody who was likely to have stolen the jacket. Some people were helpful and polite and some were not terribly happy about my intrusion into their evening. I didn't care. I just needed to get the jacket back and nothing was going to stop me. I even had an argument with the landlord who was not happy with my disturbing his patrons.

I got no information after two hours of hard work, and at closing time the situation looked hopeless. Poor George was considering buying me a new jacket just to get home and relax. As most of the people left, George turned to me and said, "I really understand that you want that jacket back, but we've tried our best, done everything we can, and it's time to accept that it's gone." Against all logic and reason, I continued to insist that I was going to get that jacket back. Just when George was on the point of looking in the yellow pages for the nearest asylum for the insane, a man came up to me and said, "I'm going to write down for you the name and address of someone who might have taken your jacket. He's a junkie who's in the habit of stealing, and he

was here last night. However, I have absolutely no evidence that he took it." I smiled, thanked the man and said to George "Let's go."

We quickly found the address and at around midnight I rang the doorbell. I could taste victory. After quite a few minutes, the lights came on and a little elderly lady answered the door wearing a dressing gown and slippers. She assured me that nobody of that name lived at that address. At that moment I saw no point in bothering her any further, so I thanked her and said goodnight. This was the time that George made his final appeal to my sense of reason. My reply was simply, "I am going to get that jacket back." If this guy didn't live at the address we were given, then we needed to find out exactly where he did live. George ran out of words to describe how crazily he thought I was behaving. As we argued the case, a taxi pulled up and a man wearing my jacket got out of it. The man who gave me the address had got the house number slightly wrong. All the anger that I'd felt at having my jacket stolen melted away, and I simply said to the man, "Give me back my jacket." He seemed a bit worried and started to make all sorts of excuses for why he had taken it. I simply took the jacket and went home a happy man. Not only did I have the satisfaction of getting my jacket back, and the marvellous opportunity to say to George, "You were ready to give in far too easily", but I had learned a lesson that virtually anything is possible if you focus hard enough on what you want. I also had a feeling that something bigger than me was in control of all this.

At this time I was on the lookout for interesting musicians. I met a guy called Pete who was a singer-songwriter from Newcastle. He had been doing some experimental writing with Keith Levene (who had departed from The Clash two years before). He played me some of his songs on the piano and they were really unusual but catchy. We started working together and he promptly changed his name to Ken Lockie (I really never understood why). We started to recruit musicians, one of whom was Marco Pirroni, a guitarist. Marco was easy to work with and a good guitarist but none of us had any idea he could write songs. He later went on to have a great deal of success with Adam and the Ants. We also found bass player Jimmy Hughes, with whom

I formed a great rhythm section. We called the band Cowboys International, signed a record deal with Virgin and started touring the UK. We built a following and eventually recorded an album called Original Sin. This was at a time when music technology was developing at an explosive pace. We started using sequencers, combining this with real instruments played in real time. I still feel they were great songs but it seems the band was ahead of its time. A whole bunch of electro-pop bands came along soon after. Ken went on to work with John Lydon and Keith Levene with PIL (Public Image Limited). A few years later, Ken was bizarrely voted 'The most obnoxious Englishman in New York'.

Whilst in the middle of the Cowboys International project, I received a telephone call from a lady I did not know. She had started a band and they needed a drummer. Johnny Thunders had recommended me. She sounded very pleasant and interesting, and so I decided to go down and spend a few hours rehearsing with them. They played very well, the songs were original and classy and they all seemed to be very nice people. We got down to discussing business and they told me that, although they had a manager, there was, as yet, no record deal and therefore no money. At the time, I was working with a band that did have a deal and, although we weren't yet selling records, we were, so to speak, higher up the ladder. I decided to reject the new offer to join on the basis that it was going backwards. I politely refused, to which they responded, "We think you're making a mistake." They were right. The lady was Chrissie Hynde and the band was The Pretenders. They were at number one in the charts in less than a year.

I left Cowboys International as we were not getting enough commercial success. Once again, Bernard Rhodes popped up and asked if I was interested in working with his favourite artist, Vic Goddard. Vic seemed to have been around from the very first days of Punk. He had formed the band Subway Sect and supported The Clash on numerous occasions. Even when Bernard was no longer working with The Clash, he would always have time for Vic who he felt was one of the most talented musicians he had ever come across. Bernard asked me to play on an album with Vic, which I was happy to do

because Vic had always intrigued me as one of the most unusual characters in the whole Punk movement. To this day I have never been able to work out what makes Vic tick. He is not the slightest bit interested in fame for its own sake and is very humble and easy to get on with, which is very unusual for any songwriter or front man.

We needed a bass player so we called up an old friend of Vic's who had always been a talented bass player and who was currently not in a band. We met in the local café and were totally shocked when he opened his mouth. This was not the same man we had known six months earlier. He told us he had taken lots of magic mushrooms (yes, the type that contained hallucinogenic substances similar to LSD). He said, in a very slow and matter of fact voice, that he hadn't played the bass for a month but he would go home and pick it up to see if he could still play. If he could, he would come along and play with us, and if he couldn't he would retire altogether. At that time this was the worst example I had seen of the damage that LSD could do. Regrettably, I have seen many others since. Getting drunk and making a fool of yourself is one thing, but permanently damaging your brain is quite another. If those people considering using LSD could meet such people it would surely dissuade them. I hope the man with the mushrooms recovered but I fear he didn't - I never saw him again.

My brother, Bryn, stepped in and played the bass and did a great job. We recorded the album quite quickly and it sounded great. There was a similarity between Vic and Ken Lockie. Although very different characters they were both very talented and both failed to achieve the commercial success that they deserved.

When you're in a band there are always plenty of girls around but I was looking for someone with whom I could have a proper conversation. I met a girl called Maxine. We got along well and started dating. She was a girl I could talk to about anything – politics, music, art, movies, etc. She enjoyed all the crazy parties but was able to keep her life together. Maxine had been working in media resources but was about to go to law school. We eventually decided to get married. During our engagement, my brother

John got married to another percussionist called Polly, with whom I got on extremely well (thank God!) and we all looked forward to the two weddings. On John and Polly's wedding day we were driving the 80 miles from London to Sudbury, when about thirty minutes into the journey my clutch failed. When this happens you can keep going but if you stop the car you cannot get started again. I drove a further 50 miles to the church without stopping. Maxine had several heart attacks on the way, but we got there just in time to hear "I do". They now have two lovely daughters, Katie and Anna. Katie followed in my footsteps to become a chiropractor and Anna is a designer. Having nieces is fantastic. It's like having kids without the expense and stress. I have always enjoyed being an uncle and, who knows? It may have been a good apprenticeship for being a father one day!

When it came to my wedding I decided to invite the whole family, which was a bit like inviting one half of London. The East End part of the family hired a large coach. The last pick-up stop for the coach was my Gran's house. She got on the coach and then suddenly exclaimed that she had to go back into the house. The 60 or so passengers waited patiently for 15 minutes, whereupon she emerged – wearing a different hat! I remember Uncle Manny commenting to her, "Who's going to look at you?" as she was then ninety-five years old. I thought it was great that she still took pride in her appearance at that age. The wedding was on July 28th 1979, which was the hottest day for five years.

We hired a vintage Rolls Royce for the day. The car only had to go about one mile but unfortunately, whilst taking Maxine to the church, it broke down. Maxine was given a lift by an elderly chap in a little Vauxhall hatchback. When we came out of the church there were two vintage Rolls Royces there, just in case. We then had a big party with my dad's band providing the music. I vividly remember my entire family waving us goodbye as we left – a very emotional experience. We spent two weeks on honeymoon on the island of Crete.

Soon after, we visited some friends in Northampton. While we were there we looked at a house and fell in love with it so we bought it and moved there. The prices there were so much cheaper as it's about 60 miles north of

London. That meant I was always the first to get home when we played north of London and the last to get home when we played south. Paul Simonon once asked me, "What's it like in Nottingham?" I replied that I had no idea. There followed a short pause, then he said, "Don't you live there?" Typical Londoner!

We wanted a dog and chose a bearded collie which we named Denis, as he was a menace. Actually he was very friendly to people but would routinely attack any other animal, regardless of its size. For me he was the cutest, friendliest animal I've ever known. He shared my life for 16 years.

One night I was driving home at 2 am, which was nothing unusual in the music business, when I ran out of petrol. I put my hazard lights on and stood by the car waving at people hoping to get a lift to the nearest gas station. I suppose being dressed in punk rock stage gear wasn't the best enticement for people to pick me up. No one stopped. I was freezing to death but realised that if I got back in the car to warm up it was even less likely anyone would stop.

Just prior to hypothermia setting in, a mini-bus with the words, "Jesus Army" written all over it pulled over. I knew nothing about these people but I certainly wasn't in a position to pick and choose. I gratefully accepted their offer of a lift, both to and from the petrol station. Of course, I realised that this was their path; they help people because Jesus did. I was expecting perhaps a speech about converting to their faith or at least a leaflet but none of that was forthcoming, just a smile and their best wishes. At the time I was struck by their kindly manner and the fact that they didn't hesitate to help someone they knew nothing about. This felt like a re-run of the Good Samaritan. I have no doubt that they are still doing that today to various grateful (and ungrateful?) people.

I got a call from Tony James, whom I hadn't seen for a while. He'd formed the band Generation X while I was working with The Clash. I decided to accept an invitation to meet with Billy Idol and Tony James with a view to joining GenX (formerly Generation X). I met the two of them at the mews house they were sharing in west London. I had seen Tony at intervals

over the last three years, as he was a good friend of Mick Jones. For some reason, I'd not yet got to know Billy Idol, who was a larger than life character who really wasn't designed for anything other than to be on a stage. Billy was very enthusiastic about me joining and had a very likeable personality. This is very important when you are thinking about joining a band, in the same way it would be important if you were joining a football team. Added to this, Tony was (and still is) the type of person who could sell sand to the Arabs. Once I agreed to join the band, our first job was to find a guitarist. We signed to the Chrysalis label and I was struck at that time by the difference in approach between Virgin and Chrysalis. Virgin's strategy seemed to be to sign up as many bands as possible in the hope that one of them made it, whereas Chrysalis would sign one band and try and make sure that they made it. Needless to say I preferred the Chrysalis approach.

We all felt that this project needed a strong manager. We were introduced to Bill Aucoin, a big-time manager who, at the time, was still managing Kiss. He was a great guy to be around: every time he came to the UK he would take you straight to a nightclub and order champagne. He had that deep confidence that comes from massive achievement. We all held him in very high regard and were sure he would bring us the big success we were after. Managers of bands are often markedly different in appearance from those they manage – this has become something of a cliché in the music business – and Bill was no exception, he bore more than a passing resemblance to John Cleese.

We must have auditioned thousands of guitarists. We couldn't believe how hard it was to find the right person. When it came to recording we had to call upon various guitarist friends to help us. We worked with Danny Kustow from the Tom Robinson Band and the late John McGeoch from Magazine, Visage, Siouxsie and the Banshees, and PIL. Eventually we found Jamie Stevenson (who was later to work with Glen Matlock, The Alarm and The Cult) to finish the album. We had discussed the idea of having Giorgio Moroder produce the album. This would have been a very unusual step for a punk band. In the event Giorgio was too busy but came back with a suggestion

that his right-hand man Keith Forsey would be perfect for it. Keith came from Ilford and had played drums on virtually everything that Moroder did, so he was no stranger to a studio. We hesitated over this choice but agreed to meet Keith. He was a very positive let's do it now kind of guy. We decided to take a chance. We started by recording the single, 'Dancing with Myself' and were very happy with the outcome.

We went on to do the album with Keith, who turned out to be a very gifted producer. He went on to produce Simple Minds and many others. If I have a perpetual deficit, it is that I am not at all visual and almost invariably fail to recognise famous people when I meet them. This can sometimes be embarrassing as it can be mistaken for arrogance. The worst example of this is when I was introduced to a woman called Diana in a nightclub and someone had to point out to me later that I'd just met Diana Ross. I met Marvin Gaye when we were recording the GenX album. He had been brought into the studio to record a radio ad. Just as he arrived there was a legal dispute about whether or not he could do the ad, as he was contracted to a record company for everything he sang. He ended up sitting on the sofa for about four hours whilst the lawyers argued. He finally went home without singing a single note, as they couldn't reach an agreement. Still, at least it gave me the opportunity to meet the great man. A few years later I was shocked to hear that he'd been shot dead by his own father.

After talking to Marvin, I decided to try out the pool table. During the recording of that album I had plenty of free time. One of the good things about being the drummer is that you can get your work done first and then relax whilst everyone else sweats. I wandered off to the recreation room, which had various machines and a pool table. There was nobody there for me to play pool with. One of the studios was undergoing an extensive building renovation so I wondered if one of the builders would be around to give me a game. An Irish guy walked in wearing jeans and a t-shirt. I asked him for a game of pool and he agreed. Whilst chatting to him over the game of pool I asked him how the work was going and he said not bad, they hoped to be finished in about three weeks. After about half an hour of playing

pool, I said to him, "Shouldn't you be getting back to work?", to which he replied, "No they're fine without me, let's have another game." I thought to myself, whoever is paying these builders will be miffed to know that one of them is playing pool all day. About an hour later, he finally announced that he should go back and do some work and then surprised me by saying that he wasn't very happy with the last guitar solo he'd played so he was going to go back and redo it. He wasn't the builder but Rory Gallagher, probably Ireland's greatest ever guitarist! A humble and incredibly charming man, he died following complications from a liver transplant and is buried in Ireland on the Clash road.

I later sat in on a meeting with our new manager, Bill Aucoin, and Chris Wright, the boss of Chrysalis. After hearing the single, 'Dancing with Myself,' Chris said, "If we can't make this single a hit then we shouldn't be in business." It wasn't a hit! When we finished the album, just about everybody loved it. Yet for some reason we couldn't understand, it just wouldn't sell. I felt we had a great team, one of the best managers in the business, a great new producer in Keith (who went on to produce many other hits) and one of the best record companies around. Nobody could explain why that album would not sell. Sometimes in life there comes a point where you just have to move on. So we split the band up and went our separate ways. I stayed in contact with Tony as we had some ideas that we felt could be developed and we had been a good team. Billy went to the USA to start again. Sadly, Bill Aucoin died recently following complications from prostate surgery.

Billy was a great character, always joking and mimicking other accents and voices. He was in love with rock'n'roll and never seemed interested in doing anything else. When we were working together we were both about 25 years old. At that time he had never taken any drugs and hardly ever seemed to get drunk. Bill Aucoin managed him and Billy quickly established himself. One would have thought that, having avoided drugs for years in the music business, by the age of 26 he was home and dry. Unfortunately this was not the case. I remember meeting up with him in 1982 when I was touring the states. He was pleased to see me but his pupils were very constricted – a common sign of heroin use.

During the time we worked together, I noticed that his heroes had been people like Elvis, John Lennon and Lou Reed – all associated to some degree with drug abuse. He seemed to subscribe to the idea that to be truly great you need to experience that stuff. He struggled for a long time with drug addiction but at least managed to keep his career going. I hope all that is behind him now, but it's not easy to get out of that trap. I remember Tony James saying to me, "Once you start on heroin, you can never completely beat the addiction." I thought that a bit harsh, but in my years of working with drug-addicted musicians, I've seen little to change that opinion. I kept hearing rumours that Topper Headon (the new drummer with The Clash) was regularly using heroin. I'd seen enough of what it did to Johnny Thunders and was never interested in trying it.

NEAR DEATH EXPERIENCE NUMBER 2

As a very optimistic person, I have always been able to laugh off failure, for instance, when we released a record and it didn't get into the charts. I was always able to say, "Never mind, the next one will make it." There came a time when life wasn't going too well for me. Not only did our record not get into the charts but I didn't have a band. I had no income and nothing coming up on the horizon. My financial responsibilities were piling up. In the face of unpaid bills, I decided I would simply roll my sleeves up and go and do some work. As a musician I didn't really have any other specialised saleable skills. I got a temporary job driving a delivery van, which wasn't particularly well paid, but at least it meant that I was keeping the wolves from the door.

Late one night, whilst making a delivery in the East End, I became aware of the presence of two men, one behind me and one at my side. The one at my side was pointing a very long thin knife at my neck and demanding money. I decided that there was no point in arguing, especially as I remembered being

told that knives were more dangerous than guns, because knives don't make lots of noise and bring unwelcome attention. Funny how such things pop into your mind at certain times. I gave them my wallet, which contained the princely sum of £5. They became angry because for some unknown reason they were certain that I had large amounts of money, either on me or in the car. As soon as the guy behind me moved into my field of vision I made my escape and although I received a knife wound in my arm I felt this was definitely preferable to one in my neck.

You do feel somewhat vulnerable when someone holds a nine-inch blade at your neck. In those situations you don't really have time to worry because you are so pumped full of adrenaline that you are running on automatic pilot. I was taught as a child that everyone has a guardian angel that looks after you. Throughout my life I have felt slightly guilty, as it would appear that my guardian angel has to work three times as hard as everyone else's. He certainly put in a full shift that evening as the eventual injuries I sustained were far milder than they might have been.

The wound I had received was small but deep, with profuse bleeding. I walked down the empty street at two-o-clock in the morning, wondering how I could call an ambulance. A large van pulled up and the driver got out to go into his house. I approached him and explained that I had just been stabbed. All I wanted was for him to call an ambulance. He said, "I'm really tired now, but if you walk to the end of the street, turn left and walk another two hundred yards you'll see a phone box." I was in no mood to stand there arguing with him so I walked to the phone box and did it myself. The ambulance came quickly and they were great.

After being patched up I was taken to the police station. I explained everything, including a good description of the main assailant, who had a massive scar down his cheek. Then the two detectives started muttering to each other. One said, "It sounds like…" then mouthed something to his colleague. The other guy said, "No, he's well over thirty and besides, he's a nutter – he would probably have killed him just for the hell of it." The first detective said, "He's actually thirty, and he may well have killed him." They

continued this conversation out of the room and came back in. They said, "We are going to show you a photo but you must never tell anyone you've seen it." I was intrigued and readily agreed. They then amazed me by showing me a photo of the guy that had just stabbed me. They explained that in order to get a conviction I would have to pick him out of an identity parade. If his lawyer knew that I'd seen that photo then the case would collapse. I told them I understood perfectly and was ready to pick him out any time. They said they'd be in touch and gave me a lift home. I had no problem with lying about having seen the photo, as there was not the slightest doubt about his identity. Also I felt he was definitely going to kill or injure innocent people so the quicker he went behind bars, the better.

Two months had gone by since I reported my attack to the police and I still hadn't heard from them, which seemed odd. I contacted them and another detective arranged to meet with me. I told him the whole story and he apologised that the night staff had not passed the case on to the day staff. I was not worried about any of that; I simply wanted this guy behind bars. He assured me that there would be no problems now and that he would contact me in a few weeks. Months later, after hearing nothing more, I again made contact with the police. This time I was told that the person I had last spoken to had left the force and they knew nothing about it. At that point I gave up on the quest for justice. It seemed that you had to be continually pestering to get anything done, and I didn't feel I had the time for that. I suspect that "Scarface" ended up in prison or dead before too long.

———

I felt at that time that my efforts to earn a living in any shape or form were being thwarted. I was also sinking further into debt, since it took several weeks to recover from the injury.

When my arm healed I still had no prospects of income from music, so I decided to go out and try to earn some money once again. This time I went to an employment agency and said, "Just give me some work to earn some money – I don't care what it is." They sent me to a huge furniture store where I stood around with lots of other guys. An enormous truck pulled up and opened its doors. It was loaded with flat-packed furniture. We unloaded these packs, forming a human chain so somebody would throw you a wardrobe, which you threw to the next guy. I had occasionally gone to a gym but only for an hour at a time. This was two and a half hours solid. I gasped with relief when a tea break was announced. I nearly choked on my tea when, after only ten minutes we had to go back to work. Tea breaks in a recording studio normally last one or two hours. By the end of the day, I felt like the truck had run over me several times. I then faced the prospect of going back for another day, and another, and another. I was constantly aware of the fact that even while doing this punishing work, I was actually still sinking into debt, (albeit more slowly than if I had not been working). It took about two weeks for me to experience a feeling of complete failure and despair. Once I had felt those feelings profoundly, I got a wonderful phone call, "We want you to come and make this album but we can only pay you three grand." I bit the caller's hand off to the shoulder and went back to doing what I did best.

The lessons learned from experiencing failure and despair tend to stay with you for the rest of your life. This is really good news because you don't want to be relearning these lessons too often. For me, one of the big lessons is that whenever I sell a product or service I am acutely aware that the purchaser may be one of the many who have to work really hard to earn that money. The vitally important point to bear in mind when it comes to failure is that although a given venture failed, that does not make you a failure.

I carried on working for a time with Tony James, who had several special gifts. He was full of enthusiasm and determination and he was a great one for knowing what was generally going on – unlike myself, usually oblivious to the world outside the band I was playing in. We did several projects together as a drummer/bass player team, helping various other bands on the way. We were

hired by Dave Dee (formerly of Dave Dee, Dozy, Beaky, Mick and Titch — a contender for the world's most ridiculous band name). Dave had a record label called Double Dee Productions. We made an album with the London Cowboys, a band formed by Steve Dior who had previously auditioned for GenX. Actually, I had thought that he should join GenX but there was a feeling with Billy and Tony that his personality would clash and perhaps they were right.

Tony and I also worked on our own stuff and he persuaded Annie Lennox, who was then between bands (after The Tourists and before The Eurythmics) to do a vocal track for us. She did a great job singing on that track but for some unknown reason that music never saw the light of day. We also helped Stiv Bators to form The Lords of the New Church. Tony later went on to form Sigue Sigue Sputnik in 1984.

———

MY COMPUTER PHASE

Towards the end of the seventies my old friend, Robin Beauchamp, was working with computers. He seemed to be enjoying himself and earning a fortune. He often told me about his work. Computers intrigued me, because they were getting more and more powerful and seemed to be taking over the planet. I had always been good at science at school and enjoyed any kind of mental puzzle. Like many musicians, I resented the fact that when you are in a band you have to be in certain places at certain times. I often missed various social events because I simply couldn't be there. Friends of mine in so-called normal jobs would simply take a day off and go to the party. This is an example of the grass appearing to be greener. I decided I would make friends with computers and try and figure out how they work.

I took an aptitude test for work in the computer industry for the sake of curiosity. This was rather like an IQ test. I got 100%, which my examiner found amusing, joking that he was always suspicious of anyone who got that mark. That gave me the confidence to take things further.

So I took some courses and found that I seemed to have a flair for programming computers. I learned two programming languages, COBOL and PLI and managed to get some programming work. I found the challenge of getting these huge machines to do what you wanted quite exciting. However, having overcome the challenge and having produced some solutions to various problems, the novelty wore off – and I stopped enjoying it. As always, as soon as I stopped enjoying it, I immediately changed direction. I got a job supporting people who were using computer programmes. This involved lots of travel, talking on the phone and lunches. This too I enjoyed at first but then again the work became routine. At that point, I realised that not only was the grass not greener – it was actually browner. At that point I returned to playing music.

It was whilst juggling both music and computers that I had a phone call from an old acquaintance.

Left:
My first photo. I later learned
how to pose much better.

Right:
My first business consulting call

Me insisting on wearing long trousers

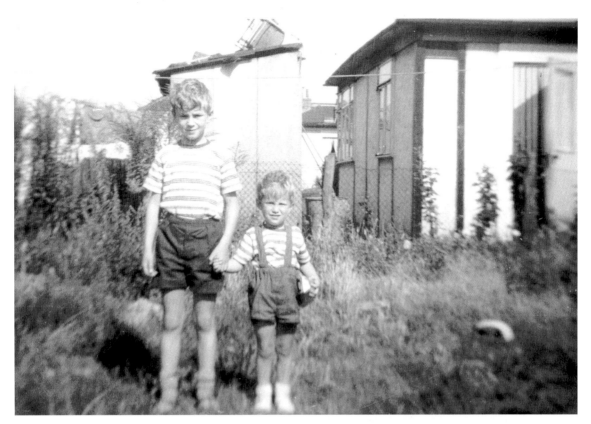

Above: Terry (left) Bryn (right) *Below: John (left) and Terry (right)*

Above: The Bill Chimes Band

Left: Bill Chimes

*Above: The Clash about to go onstage
by Maxine Chimes*

*Below: The Clash caricatures
by Michael Kloongian*

Caricature of Terry by Michael Kloongian

Above: Life on the road. L-R Terry, Joe, Kosmo by Maxine Chimes

Below: After show party L - R Billy Idol, Terry, Steve Stevens, Bill Aucoin by Maxine Chimes

CHAPTER 4
THE CLASH PART 2 (1982-83)

I want to be thoroughly used up when I die, for the harder I work the more I live. I rejoice in life for its own sake. Life is no "brief candle" for me. It is a sort of splendid torch which I have got hold of for the moment, and I want to make it burn as brightly as possible before handing it on to future generations.

George Bernard Shaw

In 1982 I received a phone call out of the blue from Bernard Rhodes asking me to meet him that very day at Marine Ices, an ice cream bar in Camden Town. I had been in contact with Bernard a couple of times over the years for odd reasons but certainly not regularly. I called Maxine to tell her what was happening and that I didn't know what Bernie wanted. She said, "There's only one reason he could have for wanting to see you so urgently." When I turned up there he was with Cosmo Vinyl whom I had met briefly before but never knew very well. He was currently the band's spokesman.

It struck me at that time that Bernard was a bit apprehensive – as if he had been sent to do a job but didn't know how to approach it. To be fair to Bernard he had never understood what motivates me, which made his job much harder. They told me that The Clash were due to play in the United States in a few days and they wanted me to join up for the tour. I'd noticed in recent press reports that Joe had gone missing. I wasn't worried about that because, in a sense, that would be quite a normal thing for Joe to do. My first question was, "Where's Joe?" They both said, "We've got him back." Joe had disappeared and holed up for a while in Paris. We briefly discussed the whole idea and Bernard's comment was that I had left too early and now was the

time to make up for that. I had to admit that, in this case, Bernie was probably right. I had wondered over the previous five years, what it would have been like had I stayed with the band. Now I had an opportunity to find out.

Some people hate sudden unplanned chaotic events but I have always enjoyed them. It would mean learning an awful lot of songs in a short space of time but I had done that many times before. I telephoned Mick later that day to discuss the idea and he quipped, "I bet you haven't got any of the albums!" to which I replied, "You've never sent me any of them!" He also said, "Well, we couldn't get Cozy Powell, could we?" (Cozy Powell was a very well known session drummer and the first person people called if they wanted a solid hard rock drummer who was a quick learner).

I had no hesitation in dropping what I was doing to take off immediately but there were two slight problems. The first was that I wouldn't have time to get a work permit for the United States; the second was that Paul was already in the USA so I would have to initially rehearse in London with Mick and Joe and catch up at the other end in New York. I met up with Joe and Mick soon after and realised there was a third problem. Because they had so many songs, they had got into the habit of changing the set every night, so each gig would be a unique experience and we wouldn't get stuck in a rut playing the same songs. From my point of view it meant memorising three times as many songs! Obviously the songs on the first album would be easy. I had, over the years, observed the band's progress but from a distance and with no attention to detail, so I had a big task on my hands – to learn 60 songs in five days. I expressed to Joe my feeling that this was a tough job and he replied, "That's ok – we're used to public rehearsals. We did one the other night." We started rehearsing with Joe on rhythm guitar and Mick playing bass. I was genuinely surprised at just how musically diverse the material had become. We bashed through a whole pile of songs and I made copious notes to aid my memory. Then we set off for the USA.

At the airport we bumped into James Honeyman-Scott, guitarist with The Pretenders, and he seemed in good spirits. When we arrived in America we were surprised to see on TV that he had died the next day of heart failure

caused by cocaine intolerance. Speaking to an apparently healthy person the day before his death makes it even more of a shock.

Because of the rush we had no time to apply for a work permit, so it was decided that I would just go into America as a tourist and get the paperwork done at a later time. This shouldn't have been a problem since English people visit America in their droves all the time. This, however, was The Clash and nothing ever seemed to go smoothly. On the flight an argument broke out between an irate older lady and some guys from the road crew. Unfortunately, when people in the rock business are told to sit down, be quiet and behave themselves they react rather badly. The more she told them off, the more they would throw things at her.

When we landed, security at the airport had been informed about the trouble-makers and there was a crowd of police and immigration officials waiting for us. The lady stood with these security people and pointed out each one of the party as they came off the plane. Despite the fact that I had had nothing to do with this lady at any time, she picked me out as being one of those responsible. The incident itself was comparatively minor and, at worst, would result in a warning. When the immigration officials looked at the details, they noticed that I had no work permit and also saw from my passport that that my stated profession was musician. So the officials saw a young, English musician with a crowd of other young English musicians and road crew, all dressed in similar clothes and on the same flight. They let all of the others go in a very short time but I was hauled in for an interview.

I realised at that point that if I told them I was here to work without a work permit I would be sent back to England and the tour would be cancelled, which would be a disaster for all concerned. I rapidly determined that the only way to handle the situation was to lie. I told them that the reason I was on the same flight and dressed the same was that I was a major fan of the band and followed them around, which they let me do as long as I behaved myself. The officials didn't believe my story for a minute but equally, it was impossible for them to disprove it. They kept saying, "Just tell us the truth and everything will be okay." I was well aware that this was one of those situations where

telling the truth would have ended in disaster. After going round in circles for two hours, they decided to let me go. The official told me he didn't believe me but he had run out of time and that if he ever saw me again without a permit I would be, "drummed out of the country!"

On arrival in New York we started rehearsals with all four of us and began to sound like a band. The road crew were mostly new guys except for The Baker who was looking after me with the drums. He hadn't changed. He would walk in bringing in a load of sandwiches and saying, "Shall I just put these in a trough in the corner?" We then commenced a full-scale American tour. Each night I went on stage with a completely different set list from the previous show and details of each song written down on a folder sitting on the bass drum. The papers in the folder would tell me what kind of rhythm the song had, what the introduction consisted of, the order of verses and choruses and what type of ending. This way, if I went blank, I would get a clue from the list.

Bernard complained to me that when I reached forward to turn the page between songs it looked from the audience as if I was reaching for a tomato sandwich! My reply was that if we had to change the set list every night I would have to have some memory aid in place, and that was that. The tour started with three shows in Asbury Park, next door to a funfair. After the first show we did lots of press interviews at the funfair. Bernard's idea was that we would all drive bumper cars around, each of us with a journalist as a passenger. When the bumper cars stopped moving, the journalist would have to jump out and let another one in. Like many of Bernard's ideas there was a lot of novelty value but it didn't really work in practice. It was too noisy and we kept getting interrupted by the cars bumping into each other.

After the second show in Asbury Park, we finished a song and I had to do a minor repair on a drum before the next song started. This only took about 30 seconds. I then looked up and to my horror saw that the other three had left the stage. I'd been so preoccupied with getting the songs right that I missed the fact that it was the last song. I had two choices – I could either sheepishly walk off, or alternatively, get the rest of the band back on stage. I

opted for the latter, so I bashed a couple of drums and cymbals, at which the audience looked on with curiosity and the other three looked at me from the wings with their jaws dropping. I then waved my arm so as to beckon them back on stage. Of course the audience gave a loud cheer and they came back for another song.

As the shows progressed, I got more used to the songs and didn't require any memory aids but I rapidly developed favourite and not-so favourite songs. I really enjoyed all of the old ones but also many of the new ones. I think 'Straight to Hell' became my favourite because it was one of the few moments in the set that I was able to sit back and enjoy the show rather than beating the hell out of the drums. It was also nice to hear the way Joe sang that song – he put much emotion into it. By the time we were halfway through the first leg of this US tour we had started discussions about further commitments. After a bit of arguing about various things I agreed to do the forthcoming UK tour and the second leg of the US tour, which would take us the rest of that year.

Just as I was getting comfortable, Joe sat me down and said he had to discuss something of the utmost seriousness. He and Cosmo informed me that the band was being sued for over a million dollars and that a private detective has been sent to serve a writ on the band. Therefore, it was crucially important that I didn't speak to anyone in a suit and must absolutely not accept a letter from anyone.

Naturally I asked who was suing us. To which they replied, "A toilet company". "You must both think I was born yesterday?" I said. You see, when you are in a band you only work for one hour a day. The rest of the time you are sitting around talking to each other, reading a book or drinking in a bar. With so much time on their hands musicians tend to spend a high proportion of it winding each other up with ludicrous stories. In other words, when you are in a band, every day is April 1st and after years of this you become hardened to it, making it more difficult to wind you up which increases the challenge so that your fellow musicians want to do it even more.

They said that the toilet company who were suing us had a 90% share of the non-blue market. To which I replied, "How the hell would you

know there is such a thing as the non-blue market?" Joe and Cosmo got quite irritated with me as I simply refused to take this story seriously. They eventually convinced me because I reasoned they would never put this much effort into it unless it was true. The album Combat Rock, which had just been released, contained a track called 'Inoculated City' with a long fade-out. Joe had seen a commercial for this toilet company on TV with an actor explaining how wonderful their product was in a really fast speaking voice. I think the company was called 'Two Thousand Flushes'. Joe had recorded this off the TV and dubbed it onto the album. When the toilet company heard the song, they thought The Clash was mocking their product. The result was that we had to avoid this private detective with his writ until our lawyer could do a deal. The deal, which took about three days to finalise, was that further copies of the album would not contain the toilet commercial and all copies containing it would be removed from the shelves. We didn't bother with this last part as we figured there was no way they could check. But we had three days of hiding from everyone we saw who was wearing a suit. When you're looking for them it is quite surprising how many people are wearing suits.

Onstage, each member of the band has their own monitor - a separate amplification system to give them the sound they want. This is especially important for singers, as they need to be able to hear themselves in order to sing in tune. Different musicians like different sounds in their monitors. Topper had been touring with the band for a long time and he used to have a large monitor with the drums turned up really loud. I, on the other hand, liked to hear the rest of the band because I knew what I was playing but needed to know what they were playing. There are no rights or wrongs about this — it is just a case of personal preference. The problem is that what you have in your monitor can affect other people.

Joe Strummer was used to hearing enormously loud drums behind him for several years. When I came back into the band in 1982, he had very little of the sound of the drums behind him. People tend to want what they are used to. He told me several times that he wanted me to hit the drums harder. I had always been fond of playing hard so I simply hit them harder. Unfortunately

this made very little difference. What would have made a difference was to put a thousand watts of amplification behind him. This was an absurd battle of wills between two proud people. If he had asked me to turn up the volume of the drums in my monitors, I would have probably cheerfully obliged. However, when someone tells a drummer to hit them harder, he will take it personally. I was hitting the drums so hard, that even though we were using the strongest drum skins on the market at that time, they had to replace the snare drum once or twice during a one-hour set because I had beaten it into a crater. Baker, the drum roadie, kept shaking his head and saying, "I've never seen anything like this before!" Looking back, I feel I was selfish because I would have got used to hearing the drums louder – instead I stuck to my guns and made his life a lot harder. It just goes to show that pride aids nothing and can do lots of damage.

I've always loved loud music but it occurred to me that if you listen to it long enough you would go deaf. To me there was nothing cool about being deaf. I decided I would try and play music on stage with earplugs. To my amazement, I found that you actually hear better with earplugs. The reason is that very loud music gives your eardrums such a brutal bashing that they go numb and your ears ring for hours afterwards. Wearing earplugs protects the eardrums against the severe shockwaves enabling you to hear with much greater clarity through the whole range of frequencies. Once I realised this I always wore earplugs.

The wisdom of wearing earplugs was confirmed to me when I went on stage and played a whole show. We went back for an encore and then retired to the dressing room to get changed. I pulled out the earplugs and then we were told that the audience was insisting on one more encore, which we decided to go back and do. I forgot to put back the earplugs. The noise was totally unbelievable to me. It felt like being strapped down and tortured. Of course, when you're playing drums you are quite unable to put your hands over your ears, which I would dearly have loved to do. The experience taught me the value of the earplugs in retaining my hearing. There is no shortage of deaf ex-rock musicians in this world.

Joe never lost his sense of humour and you never quite knew what to expect next with him. We were playing a gig in America in an indoor theatre that had about 50 doors, when he said, "You people standing by the door at the back, could you turn the lights on?" The lighting engineer took the hint from Joe and turned about 100.000 watts of house lights on and the whole room was suddenly illuminated. Half of the audience were looking around the room to see where this light switch was.

At some stage, a new tradition appeared whereby the audience would throw their clothes onto the stage. We had no idea where this came from but the roadies would gather up all of the clothes and bring them backstage after the show and, if there was anything there that one of us liked, we would start wearing it. On one occasion somebody threw a pair of shoes on the stage (I presume they went home barefoot). When you are playing with a big lightshow, as we did, you can't see anything but the lights when you look out into the audience. When the shoe hit me in the face I had absolutely no warning it was about to happen — it was like being slapped by the invisible man. It isn't that painful but it is a surprise and you find yourself wondering when the next one is going to come. Saying that, generally, drummers have it easy when it comes to missiles or spitting, as they are further back and surrounded by equipment.

During that American tour I was reading the life story of Ramana Maharshi, an Indian saint who died in the 1950s. My brother John had lent it to me. I shared parts of the story with Joe who seemed intrigued but eventually dismissed the idea of spiritual development as incompatible with life on the road with a rock band. I didn't agree with him but never managed to persuade him.

About this time I did a course in meditation, which is an oxymoron — meditation is something that you do rather than talk about, but as with everything, you have to start somewhere. I had already been doing it for some weeks whilst touring the USA with the Clash. Although I was new to meditation I had the feeling that I was really onto something. It seemed to me that if everyone in the world were to do this they would be far healthier

and relationships between people would be vastly improved. Obviously, persuading everybody in the world to meditate would be no small task. You tend to start with those nearest to you. I tried with the other guys in the band but they didn't seem particularly interested. They didn't put it down in any way – I just got the impression that they all thought I was a bit weird and it was fine for me but not for them. With hindsight perhaps I should have tried harder but we were very busy and all sorts of dramas were unfolding. This is the big paradox about meditation – those that need it most do it least; and for those doing it – the times when you need it the most, you do it the least.

Later that year I was returning from a US tour on Air Canada in business class. It was a great flight but it's not fair to compare one airline in business class to another in economy. I decided that since I was stuck there for the next seven hours and I was in a comfortable seat there was absolutely no reason not to do some meditation. I went into my usual routine but this time the results were quite different. The experience is very difficult to describe because, quite simply, it was different from any other I had ever had. Firstly, I became completely unaware of my body. I felt as though I was in an ocean of blackness with no boundaries between me and the seat, the seat and the plane, the plane and the rest of the universe. I was totally immersed in an infinite sized vat, which consisted of nothing and everything at the same time. That description might sound peculiar but it is the nearest I can get to the experience in words. Another feature was that there seemed to be no time, past, present or future – It felt as if I'd stepped outside the whole realm of time and space. I felt very comfortable there and also I was aware of a feeling of limitless, unconditional love. I was in absolutely no hurry to return to "normal". I stayed in that zone for quite a while, but as I said there was no sense of time. It could have been anything between five minutes and three hours, I really couldn't gauge it.

I didn't tell anybody about the experience at the time and although I got up and went through customs, etc, I don't think I returned to my usual self for a couple of days. I have had several similar experiences over the years but they don't always come when you would like them to. I was reminded of

this when I watched the film *The Chronicles of Narnia*. There is a scene near the end when the children have returned from Narnia to their normal lives and the old man of the house sort of winks knowingly. It's obvious that he's been there too but, like them, he can't control it.

During that year there was a gradual but clear change in my values as well as my attitude to fame. When we were teenagers my band-mates and I were all obsessed with the aim of making it big. Nothing else ever came close in importance to that goal. The others still seemed to be that way but I was increasingly feeling that quite a lot in life is more important than fame and success. It didn't stop me working hard as that was a long-term habit. It just occurred to me during particular conversations that there was a gap opening up between the others and myself – a different gap from the one I had experienced five years earlier.

When we returned to LA there was a big party and I missed breakfast, so I went for a walk and came back at about 11.30 a.m. As I walked through the lobby of the hotel, Pip, our lighting engineer, happened to be in the bar. He shouted over, "Would you like a drink?" I said yes, as this had become an ingrained habit, so he ordered me a Tequila Sunrise. The measures in America are larger. I drank it on an empty stomach and went to my room. I felt suddenly very tired so I lay down for a few minutes. I woke up six hours later in the dark, feeling exhausted and with a terrible headache. I realised that I had just wasted a whole day for the sake of one drink. I decided from that moment that I would never drink alcohol again. I was twenty-six, just before the traditional age of rock death! These types of decision do not really occur on the spur of the moment but are a result of previous experiences adding up. I had seen plenty of lives ruined by alcohol and, whilst you can get away with drinking 10 pints of beer as a 19-year-old, it's really not the kind of habit you want to continue into middle age. People said, "I'll give you two weeks before you start again." It's been thirty years now and I am thinking about starting to drink again when it gets to forty years!

When we reached Colorado, we played in a venue called Red Rocks Amphitheatre. This place is made out of natural rock that happens to form

the right shape for a 10,000-seat venue. I remember standing there and being quite overawed by the size of the rocks. Joe and I wondered what this had been used for 5,000 years earlier. We decided that an Indian Chief or High Priest would have used it for performing a ritual or ceremony. I sat down to chat with Joe and he suddenly blurted out, "I just want to know one thing," – he often started conversations with this opening gambit – "How can you say I'm not going to sleep with any other woman for the rest of my life?" It's impossible to tour with a band and not know all about each other's personal life. Joe had noticed that I was not taking advantage of the fact that girls make themselves available when you tour. I explained that I had tried all that in the past and it never seemed to bring happiness. Furthermore, AIDS had just reared its ugly head. Not much was known about it then apart from, 'If you sleep with an infected person there's no cure and you die'. I don't know if I made any sense to Joe but he never asked me again. I tried to bring my wife Maxine with me on as many trips as possible but it was quite expensive because of the large number of scheduled flights.

When I joined the Clash in 1976, Joe Strummer and Mick Jones had already become vegetarians. I remember Mick telling me that when I eat meat I am eating fear. My answer was that it was ridiculous to accuse me of eating an emotion. Joe told me I would never eat meat if I ever worked in a slaughterhouse (which he had). Neither of these arguments persuaded me in any way because they made me defensive. A year or so later I was at a Greek restaurant with Billy Idol and he ordered a salad kebab – a selection of salad and vegetables with humus in pitta bread. I had my usual meat kebab. As I watched Billy tucking into this delicious-looking salad kebab, I thought how nice it would be to eat without worrying about whether the contents had any unsavoury parts of an animal (such as lips and eyes) or any bits of gristle (which I always hated). After that experience I resolved to become a vegetarian and have been one ever since. The point here is that if you want to convert somebody to your point of view, attacking them seems to make them argue with you and dig deeper into position, whereas if you show them by example they are more likely to follow.

In 1982, all four of us in The Clash were, to some extent, vegetarian. When we ordered our food it sounded like a Monty Python sketch, as Paul would eat chicken but no red meat, Mick would eat no meat but would eat seafood, Joe would eat seafood but no dairy produce and I would eat no dairy, seafood or meat. The caterers nearly always got it wrong and, looking back, I find it bizarre that we didn't just write it all down and be done with it. I had a similar experience years later with Hanoi Rocks when we weren't just ordering vegetarian food but also dishes without nuts or mushrooms because of allergies. The tour manager, Mick Staplehurst, asked to be called over when we ordered our food. He wasn't interested in the food but he just wanted to see the face of the waiter when we started to order.

So many of the greatest figures in human history have been vegetarians that I find it quite impossible to resist the urge to quote a few of them here:

"Nothing will benefit human health and increase chances for survival of life on Earth as much as the evolution to a vegetarian diet."

Albert Einstein

"As long as man continues to be the ruthless destroyer of lower living beings he will never know health or peace."

Pythagoras

"While we ourselves are the living graves of murdered beasts, how can we expect any ideal conditions on this earth?"

George Bernard Shaw

"I have from an early age abjured the use of meat, and the time will come when men such as I will look on the murder of animals as they now look on the murder of men."

Leonardo da Vinci

"If you have men who will exclude any of God's creatures from the shelter of compassion and pity, you will have men who will deal likewise with their fellow men."

St. Francis of Assisi

Steven Wright, the American comedian, said,

"If we aren't supposed to eat animals, then why are they made of meat?" This is much too deep a question for me so I will leave you to make your own mind up.

We did the UK tour and when we played London I met Topper again during the afternoon. To me he didn't seem to have changed much. We discussed the horrors of learning 60 songs in five days but not anything about his departure from the band. The two of us seemed to be destined to meet every year or so. I saw him recently at a Clash Bash (that's what Clash parties are called). Someone asked to take a photo of the two of us. It was funny to think that of all the thousands of photos we'd both had taken, this was the first and only time we'd been photographed together.

People in successful bands tend to develop huge egos, which can be very disappointing for fans when they meet them. During the UK tour, we got a Volvo hire car. Volvos are safety-mad and this car had child locks, which meant you couldn't open the door from the inside. We arrived at the show and there was a crowd of fans waiting outside. The driver jumped out and ran around to open the door for Joe Strummer. Whereupon someone in the crowd shouted "Oh, no! He's even got a chauffeur now!" Things are not always what they seem.

We played several nights at London's Brixton academy. We always had a large guest-list but this time it got really out of hand. I remember Cosmo laughing, having just heard one of the guests say, "But that can't be the queue for the guest-list." The queue for the guest list was longer than the one for regular tickets. On one of the nights we had the Burundi Drummers supporting us, Africans in traditional costumes, with huge drums and spears. I can still picture the stunned faces of those punks at the front looking wide-eyed at these drummers waving spears at them.

Next we returned to the USA for the rest of the tour. I was in a bar in Boston with The Clash and a big American guy walked over to us and said, "You've got to get out of my country, and if you don't agree with me I'll pull your ears off!" We wondered what the hell he was talking about. We eventually realised that he was referring to British troops getting out of Ireland. Cosmo Vinyl confronted the man, telling him that he had no problem with British

troops leaving Ireland but that the British were in Ireland before the white man colonized America. So if the British had to leave Ireland then the white man should leave America for the Indians. The guy walked away, calmer and somewhat confused.

At some point, we got a call from a press agent informing us that Playgirl magazine had recently produced a list of the ten sexiest men in the world. Paul Simonon was on that list. Paul's immediate reaction was one of complete disdain. In fact he angrily brushed aside any attempt by journalists to even discuss it. While he was busy saying it was absolute nonsense, the rest of us were secretly wishing that it had been us. Paul's patience was about to be tested a great deal more.

We were preparing to go onstage for an open-air concert in New York. A guitarist plays with a small plastic triangle called a pick or plectrum. Guitarists are always dropping these picks, and need a ready supply of new ones. The solution we had always used was to put a piece of double-sided tape on the amplifier and stick about a dozen picks to the tape so they could be quickly and easily retrieved. We had a new guy on the road crew who was eager to impress. He came up with a new idea that he had carefully tested. The idea was to use a spray adhesive on the front of the amp and stick the picks directly on the amp. This was quicker and less messy. The idea was good but there was one problem. He left the can of spray adhesive in the dressing room right next to the hairspray. You can guess what happened next. Paul sprayed his hair with the glue. Hairsprays come in light hold, firm hold and extra firm hold. The spray adhesive was extra, extra firm and did not produce the desired effect! When he realised what had happened he was not a happy bunny.

When people are under pressure they often focus on the problem rather than the outcome. Needless to say we were under great pressure! Somebody suggested shampooing the glue off quickly, which we tried. This had the effect of turning the glue green and had no impact on its stickiness. Someone then suggested methylated spirits, which we had used for cleaning guitars. This turned the victim's hair more of a blue colour and again had no effect on the stickiness. We were running late, and the problem was still looking

hopeless when the promoter poked his head into the room and said "You boys had better get on stage now – you're late and the audience has been waiting too long." I think the door was slammed in his face before he could finish the sentence. As the pressure mounted we focused harder and harder on the problem but couldn't come up with a solution.

Maxine came in to find out what the delay was. She had been outside chatting with Billy Idol and couldn't understand what could possibly be holding us up. Since she had not spent the last half an hour focusing on the problem, her focus was "How can we get the band on the stage?" Over the angry shouting match that was going on between all of us, she calmly uttered these few words; "Why don't you wear a hat?" As these words left her lips, silence fell and everyone's eyes moved to the hat that Paul had been wearing when he arrived and then back to Paul. Everyone simultaneously shouted "Yes!" Within five minutes we were on stage performing. Incidentally, it was a great performance; because we were all pumped full of adrenaline by the time we finally started. What's more, a thunderstorm raged all through the gig, in perfect alignment with the mood of everyone on the stage. The audience was saturated by the end of the first song, so they just couldn't get any wetter. We played White Riot as a second encore during which the lightning really went crazy – perfect!

While in America, The Clash played the TV show, *Saturday Night Live*. We were told at the time that it was the most watched TV show in the world. It was unusual in that everything went out live rather than pre-recorded. This is much less safe but more exciting. There were lots of comedy sketches in the show and we asked if our latest song, 'Rock the Casbah', could be played on a ghetto blaster as an incidental in one of the sketches. This was refused on the grounds that it had all been scripted and rehearsed so it was too late to change anything. We were a bit miffed about that so we thought we would do it ourselves.

A cunning plan was hatched. We would have the new song lined up on a ghetto blaster, which would be thrown to Joe during a pause in the song 'Should I Stay or Should I Go?' We would all stop playing and listen

to a 15-second clip of 'Rock the Casbah' and use that song as our cue to start playing again. We also had a minder posted in the control room so that the engineers could be stopped from turning us off. Like so many plans, it sounded like a really good idea at the time. Here was the problem though; we had all grown up with the old cassette machines, which worked on mechanical controls so that when you pressed pause it would stay paused until you clunked the pause button again. The machine we had with us was from a new generation that had electronic or logic controls. If you press pause on these it will stay paused for about 15 minutes and then just stop. At the crucial moment we all stopped playing and the roadie threw the ghetto blaster to Joe who pressed the pause button…

All four of us looked on in stunned silence waiting for the music that never came. We had no clearer idea about what would happen next than any of the other 25 million people watching. The gap was probably no more than three or four seconds but we all had that strange feeling of time standing still. We were all in a state of full present-time consciousness, at least for the moment. Someone took the initiative by singing the next line and we all responded by jumping back into the song together. During the last couple of choruses, as it sank in to each of us that we'd got away with it, we started laughing. For weeks afterwards on tour people would ask what we had been laughing at. They all thought that the silent ghetto blaster stunt had some deep hidden meaning. The TV crew were definitely not amused and were very cold with us afterwards. The only one who seemed to find it funny was Eddie Murphy, who was a guest presenter on the show that week.

Walking into the dressing room one day we were all delighted to see a whole set of cartoon drawings depicting each of us in cartoon form. The artist was Michael Kloongian, who later did a fabulous cartoon of me with a 'combat drum-kit' that was a converted tank.

Later on the tour, Cosmo suddenly popped up with some news: 'The Who' were about to embark on a record-breaking American tour and had asked that The Clash support them. Cosmo seemed a bit nervous as if he half expected us to refuse. In the event everybody seemed to think it was a good

idea, so we said yes and changed plans accordingly. This meant we would be staying in America a bit longer than expected. The schedule was reworked and we included some dates that we would play in between The Who shows. This was because it took more than 24 hours to move all of the equipment from one stadium to another.

The first time I played in front of a very large audience, we were about to go on stage in front of 80,000 people, which is a bit daunting when you have previously only played to a maximum of about 30,000.

Cosmo Vinyl popped into the dressing room and announced, "I've got Mick Jagger outside and I'm going to bring him in." He looked at everyone's face to get their reaction. There was vague nodding and shrugging of shoulders, which meant, "Okay — bring him in!" Part of the reason for the reticence was that The Clash had never been comfortable with hanging around with people just because they were famous and in fact avoided doing so. For instance, when Billy Gibbons, the guitarist from ZZ Top asked Cosmo if he could come up on stage and jam with the Clash, Cosmo had told him, "Only if you shave your beard off." I felt bad when I heard that, as he is one of the world's greatest guitarists and probably would have thought that reply quite odd. Furthermore, The Clash had penned the words, 'No Beatles, Elvis or the Rolling Stones', in the song '1977'. Still, that was then and this was now.

Mick Jagger came into our dressing room, apparently aware that this was our first show in front of such a large audience. He was very kind, and told us about some of his experiences in front of such audiences. He concluded that when you have played a few of these big shows, they are no different from the small ones. He was absolutely right and we soon got used to it. I commented after to the others that he was a nice guy, but his girlfriend was a bit young for him. I was later informed that she was his teenage daughter!

Bob Dylan came to a couple of shows and came backstage afterwards. I was never sure whether it was him or his kids that were interested in The Clash. He seemed incredibly introverted to me but then that's the way with lots of performers. He spent a lot of time talking to Joe about lyrics.

It was during The Who tour that Don Letts filmed the video for the song 'Should I Stay or Should I Go?' We had hired some vintage Cadillacs for the tour because we felt that it looked more special turning up in a fifties car. While we were travelling to Shea Stadium (sadly now demolished) in New York in an open-top Cadillac, Don Letts, who was making the video, filmed us from another car. So many people have said to me since that time that we all looked so miserable in that car. The answer was that we were damned near freezing to death and saying to each other, "Whose idea was this?" After we got the first couple of stadium gigs out of the way, the idea of playing to 100,000 people became quite routine. I remember Joe asking me, "How many people does this place hold?" while driving on the way to Shea stadium. When I told him 70,000 he quipped, "Pah! That's nothing!" and laughed.

As a teenage drummer growing up in London I had always admired the band Santana and enjoyed listening to their music. It was a shock to find we were playing in California with Santana as our warm-up band. It was great to meet the legendary guitarist Carlos Santana himself, who was very friendly and humble. I'm delighted to see his recent massive success with a whole new generation of fans.

One of the extra dates put in between The Who concerts was at Kent State University. They didn't have a changing room in the hall so they gave us the gym to change in, which was fine by us. In the gym there was a large silver bowl containing the white powder that gymnasts put on their hands before leaping about. I had a photograph taken of myself next to this bowl. Later back in England, I showed various people the photograph and told them that this was the stash of cocaine that The Who had in their changing room! It's amazing how many people fell for it when you think about it – that quantity would have had a street value of about half a million dollars.

Bernie Rhodes can be said to have created The Clash. Of course, he could have done nothing on his own but there again the band would not have existed without him. Bernie was incredibly determined and quite insightful. He could also be the most irritating man on the planet. I had more rows with him than anyone else in the early days and that was a major factor in my

decision to leave (the first time). When I returned in 1982, we got on much better and seemed to hardly row at all. This amused the other guys who, at one point, started to sing a new song which was Paul McCartney's 'Ebony and Ivory' with the words altered to 'Bernie and Terry, living in perfect harmony'. This was possibly the closest I've ever come to committing murder.

By November, everyone was feeling a bit exhausted after nearly a year of solid touring. I think these days most modern managers would tell a band to go off and have a 6-month holiday but holidays were something we never really did. However, we did agree to play a festival in Jamaica called Sun Splash, featuring a strange variety of bands including The Grateful Dead and The Beach Boys. I made a fool of myself on the first day as I went to have a look at the stage and see what was going on. There was a really good band of middle-aged session musicians playing and then a lady, who was very casually dressed, jumped up on the stage and sang a couple of songs. I remarked to a couple of the road crew that she had a really good voice and perhaps it wasn't too late for her to be discovered. The guy I was talking to rolled his eyes and another one tapped me on the shoulder and told me she was Aretha Franklin. I suppose that gig in Jamaica was more like a holiday than work and we were especially pleased when we bumped into a band we had worked with extensively, The Beat – called The English Beat when in America because there was an American band also called The Beat. I remember chatting to the singer, Dave Wakeling, with a couple of our road crew. Some very funny stories came up. The one that stuck in my mind concerned the habit Mick had of checking into a hotel and saying, "Could I please have a room at the other end of the hotel and on a different floor from him?" – pointing at Topper. Then he would turn to him and say, "No offence!"

When we emerged from our hotel to leave, each of us as usual carried our own cases. Waiting outside the same hotel were The Beach Boys. One of the Beach Boys said to Cosmo Vinyl, "I can't believe this band is carrying their own cases!" Cosmo replied, "If you can't carry your own case then you're f*c**d!" At precisely that moment, the Beach Boys' roadie popped up, saying, "I've loaded all the cases, shall we go?"

Being live on stage with a band is a very special experience. I don't really know what to compare it to but I would imagine it is similar to playing sport in a team where you try to get everyone in the team facing the same way and doing their best for each other. Sometimes a sports team will play brilliantly with lovely flowing moves and spectacular displays of skill. The same team can go out the following week and play like amateurs. There is a sense in both music and sport that the main aim is to get the mind out of the way. When you are trying too hard and your mind keeps worrying about the outcome, you get a poor performance. When your mind is quiet and the music or sport simply flows by itself – that is when you get the best performance. Therefore an important part of the job of the manager of a band or a sports team is to create an environment in which the players are purely focussed on giving their best performance without any other concerns or worries. That is a very difficult job and explains why people who are good at it get paid a lot of money.

Joe Strummer in particular was quite unpredictable on stage. I thought this was a good thing as I have a dread of routine. Towards the end of my time with The Clash I distinctly remember one performance when Mick was making lots of peculiar sounds from his guitar. These magic boxes (sound effects) for guitarists were getting much cleverer at that time and Mick was enjoying experimenting. This was irritating the hell out of Joe, who thought that such activity was the domain of the Pink Floyds of this world and had no place on stage with The Clash. This was at the time when the tension between the two of them had reached its peak, for all sorts of reasons.

At one point Joe looked up at the ceiling and screamed a very long and loud expletive. I have absolutely no idea how many of the fans were aware of what was really going on then but I imagine it was a very small percentage. Just after that Joe ran over to Mick and put his hand on the strings of Mick's guitar to stop the sound. This was a line he had never crossed before and came as a surprise to everyone. Nothing was said afterwards – it was as though we all pretended it had never happened. Then over breakfast the next morning Mick gave me a sidelong glance and said, "Did you see what he did last night?" This was probably the time to come up with some words of wisdom

but I couldn't seem to find them. I just said, "Yes, I saw it." At this time I was struggling to find a way to reconcile the split in the band but I think it had been many years building up and even with the benefit of hindsight there is probably nothing I could have said to make much difference.

Years later Mick Jones said in an interview that we worked way too hard for all those years with never any rest or holiday. He went on to say that these days that would never happen and we would have been sent away to rest and enjoy ourselves and then come back to make another album. It was certainly true that we were worked too hard and were under constant pressure for a very long time. It felt to me like Bernie was trying to get the band as far as he could in a short time before it blew apart. There's no doubt that bands that last a long time make the most money. However, looking back now I find it impossible to imagine The Clash any differently than working constantly under enormous pressure with everyone pushed to the limits. I just don't think it could have been any other way. In fact to have lasted over seven years doing that is remarkably more than anyone could have reasonably expected. Lots of people were very sad at The Clash splitting up. This is understandable if they were fans of the band, but it was that very intensity that attracted them to the band. In other words, there are plenty of bands without the intensity that last a very long time, but is that really what you want? Maybe you can't have it both ways.

That show in Jamaica was to be my last with The Clash. During the preceding three months or so, there had been tremendous tension building between Mick on the one hand and Joe and Paul on the other. I can never really figure out which of the two of them was more upset with Mick: Paul claimed he was but Joe seemed more vocal about it. Most bands experience a certain amount of this type of thing since being in a band is like being married to several people at once. Facing the audience and critics together can bring you very close but can also drive you to murder. At several points Joe and Paul had discussed the possibility of The Clash without Mick. I never really took that idea seriously, regarding it in the same way that men talk about murdering their wives without any real intention of doing so. It was

quite late in the day that I realised they were actually serious. I also saw that while I can be a very persuasive person, nothing I was able to say was going to make any difference – there was too much history between them.

When a band splits up nobody around them wants it to happen. Friends and relatives can no longer get free tickets, casual acquaintances can no longer boast that they hang out with famous people and the various record company execs and agents lose their Christmas bonus. More importantly, the fans feel a tremendous sense of loss, almost as if somebody has died. I have real sympathy for this as I have seen it many times but the fact is that when it's over, it's over. I moved on to the next phase of my life, Mick went off to form a new band called Big Audio Dynamite, and Joe and Paul found two new guitarists and a drummer, the group to be billed as the new Clash with a new album. I can understand why they tried but I felt it was a mistake right from the first. Then I heard that the album was produced by Bernie Rhodes, which to me sounded a bit too close to The Beach Boys, who had one of their albums produced by their psychiatrist. I have never listened to the album and probably never will. I prefer to think of The Clash as they were during 1982.

It seems I'm the first person from The Clash to write a book. Joe said on several occasions, "If any of us write a book it should be called "The Ugly Truth about The Clash." I think he might have been a touch over-sensitive about the most negative aspects of the band.

This might have been a good time for a career change but I still craved the addictive buzz that can only be satisfied by a large audience of rock fans. I was not ready to stop drumming yet. Furthermore, I was getting excited at the thought of bigger drum kits and bonkers drum solos. Fortunately, I was soon to meet and work with some of the musicians I had listened to as a 15-year-old.

CHAPTER 5
HANOI ROCKS
& BLACK SABBATH

"Action may not always bring happiness; but there is no happiness without action."

Benjamin Disraeli

When The Clash, as I knew it, was finally over, I had a conversation with Joe about my future. At that time I voiced the idea that I might leave the music industry completely. He was deeply shocked at the very thought of this and told me I was crazy. He expounded his idea that the skills I had were like those of a highly specialised industrial fitter: only a few people in the world have that skill and I would enjoy a great deal of income and privilege by selling it. If I left the music business I would be no different from anyone else and I would regret it. I tried arguing with him that being in a band is no different from any other role in life. It has its good side and bad side. The grass may or may not be greener on the other side but it would definitely be different.

Then I remembered Joe once telling me that he couldn't understand why Topper started taking hard drugs when he was playing in a successful band and even writing songs. That statement genuinely shocked me. As if being in a successful band meant you would never need to look elsewhere for comfort or pleasure. Fame can bring many benefits but it can also be a terrible trap for the ego, especially if you start believing your own press and your own fans. You can't really buy fame so people tend to over-value it. Having fame is useful only inasmuch as it shows you profoundly that it is a mirage – it's not real. That's why famous musicians rarely turn up to the after show

party – they know it's all nonsense. Andy Warhol's idea of everyone having 15 minutes of fame wouldn't work – it would be like giving everyone just enough heroin to get them addicted. Reality TV shows feed off this lie that fame brings happiness, which is why I can't watch them.

After The Clash, I felt like I'd been around the block and got the t-shirt. However, as it turned out I still had a few more years of music left in me, before building up the courage to make the jump.

One night, I was sitting at home, watching the Oscars on TV. There were people like Cary Grant and Elizabeth Taylor saying, "Thank you, I love you all", as they always do. Then suddenly on walks my old producer, Keith Forsey, to pick up an Oscar, I nearly fell off my chair. It turned out that he co-wrote the song, 'What a Feeling' with Irene Cara that was used in the movie, *Flashdance*, and won the Oscar for the best film music that year.

Not long after that, I talked to my old friend, the late, great Johnny Thunders. He asked me to join him on a UK tour alongside another band called Hanoi Rocks, from Finland. During the UK tour, the two bands shared top billing. This is unusual, but the two sets of musicians had great respect for each other. Thunders and myself would finish a performance with half of Hanoi Rocks on the stage playing some crazy improvised extravaganza. Johnny was a truly great musician who never really reaped the rewards of his work. My personal opinion is that, at some deep level, he was afraid of success. Whenever record companies came calling, which they frequently did, he would screw things up by taking drugs and vomiting everywhere, which would always frighten them off. I then toured Scandinavia with Thunders. Upon my return I received the shocking news that Razzle, the English drummer in Hanoi Rocks, had been killed in California. He had gone out to a liquor store with Vince Neil from Motley Crue. Driving drunk and speeding, Neil crashed the car. Razzle was taken to hospital and pronounced dead on arrival. He was 24 years old.

Whilst digesting that terrible news, I had to have my wisdom teeth taken out. There was a long waiting list but was told I could jump the queue

if I were willing to have it done during the Christmas holidays, to which I agreed. I was sitting in the hospital when I received a call from Richard Bishop who was co-managing Hanoi Rocks. The band had agreed to play a live TV show that was part of a Europe-wide festival called Europe-a-Go-Go and was to go out live to 200 million people. It was felt that it should go ahead as a tribute to Razzle. They needed someone to step in and play the drums, but he'd have only five days to learn the songs. I said I'd be delighted to step in and do the job and that five days was plenty of time. Unsurprisingly, this gave me a strange feeling of déjà vu. They undertook to send some tapes over by messenger so I could get started the next day. Two hours later I went down for my operation.

In the early hours of the next morning, I woke from my general anaesthetic with the feeling that all the surgeons had taken turns at kicking me in the head. I staggered to the bathroom and turned on the light. There followed probably the biggest shock I have ever had. Staring back at me from the mirror was a guy I had never seen before. He looked like an orang-utan, with grossly inflated cheeks. It took me quite a while to assure myself I wasn't dreaming. When I was sure that this was in fact my face, I thought, " Great! I'll be playing live on stage to 200 million people, looking like a giant demented hamster on steroids." Worse than that, the music Hanoi Rocks plays makes Guns'n'Roses' stuff sound like a lullaby. Just what you want to listen to when your head feels like it's going to split open any minute.

When I got to the first rehearsal I had gone from looking like a giant hamster to just an orangutan. The rest of the band thought it was hilarious. Hanoi Rocks rehearsed at a louder volume than any other band I had seen — perfect when you have a throbbing headache and aching jaws. Apart from the pain, I found playing with these guys quite enjoyable. I had a reasonable grasp of the songs by the time we went to Finland a couple of days later. I had never been to Finland before and no one warned me about the temperature. It was January and Helsinki was at -30 degrees C. When I complained about the cold they told me how lucky I was — in the North of the country it was -50, a temperature that my brain could scarcely comprehend.

When it came to the live concert, before 200 million people, there was a minor inconvenience. We were going to play a set lasting just under an hour but they couldn't (or wouldn't) tell us which two songs would be broadcast. Once again it was my destiny to memorise a lot of songs in a very short space of time. I really didn't want to screw up the two songs that were going to be broadcast and it would have been really handy to know which two they were going to be. I was told they wouldn't know until the time came. As it was I had to make sure that all of the songs were learned perfectly. I was grateful for the invention of the Walkman at that time.

I got through learning the songs by sheer determination. By applying ice packs to my face, I managed on the night to look almost normal. When these little problems arise, the best course of action is to look beyond the obstacle to the goal ahead and just get there. You can watch those songs now on YouTube.

HANOI ROCKS – GOING STEADY

Sam Yaffa, the bass player, left the band after a disagreement with the guitarist, Andy McCoy. It seems they were both in love with the same girl – never a good idea when you're in a band together.

After we got through the chaos of Europe A-Go-Go, they asked me to join the band, which is the rock and roll equivalent of going steady after the first couple of dates. I agreed to join and we started rehearsing the new set. We decided to try out the live show in Poland, which was still under the iron fist of Soviet rule – if we screwed up there no one would really know about it. We auditioned bass players and found Rene Berg, a very creative man, if not a little eccentric. With Rene on bass, Hanoi Rocks toured Poland. We went all over the country in a large coach with the road crew and a Polish hard rock band that supported us. This was in the days of communism, which seemed very strange to us. For instance, if you ate in a restaurant there would be as many waiters as customers. None of them, however, moved very fast. If you

went to a shop, there would be no more than twenty or thirty items for sale and they all seemed ridiculously cheap.

There was a strange man in the Polish crew with whom I never had a conversation because he didn't speak any English. He was there to provide pyrotechnics. This was before the tedium of health and safety regulations had reached Poland. His fireworks were home-made — by a lunatic. The problem was that we had no idea when these bombs would go off in performance, and every now and then there would be a huge explosion. We would look over to where the sound had come from and he would be sitting there with a huge satisfied smile on his face. A part of me misses those days when you could do virtually anything you wanted — that guy would not last ten seconds in England today!

During that Polish tour I was in a bar and noticed that they had alcohol-free beer and veggie burgers. I ordered one of each and when my band mates joined me they were horrified to see me drinking beer and eating a burger! These were the same people who had made fun of me for ages as a health nut. They immediately set about trying to persuade me to go back to non-drinking vegetarianism! I let them suffer for 20 minutes or so and then revealed the truth. It struck me then that most people don't care what you do or don't do, but are genuinely horrified if you make big changes.

The guitarist's name was Nasty Suicide. He and I became great friends. Once in Poland we stopped at a level crossing and were advised that we would be waiting here for 20 minutes so those who wanted to could stretch their legs. There was a party going on in a garden right next to the coach, with a band playing. Our two guitarists, Andy McCoy and Nasty Suicide, went over and played guitar with the band and we all joined the party. They were both very skilled at flamenco guitar and impressed the locals. Eventually the driver gave us a call and we all got back on the bus.

There were about 50 people on the bus, as there were several bands on this tour, with several road-crew members. About two hours later, the photographer who was travelling with us, Justin Focus, woke me up. He

begged me to believe what he was telling me, which was that Nasty was not on the bus. I replied, "He must be". Justin said, "You're the only sober person on this bus so you have to check, because I'm sure he is not on here." I checked and sure enough Nasty was missing. He obviously didn't get back on the bus with the rest of us. I told the driver, which took some considerable time as he didn't speak English. We were only half an hour away from our destination and turning back was not really an option. When we arrived at the hotel, I immediately sent a cab back for Nasty and we all tucked into breakfast. About 8 hours later, Nasty arrived, looking somewhat bedraggled. He had been wandering around in the Polish countryside with no idea where he was going, where he had come from and totally unable to speak the language. God only knows how the cab driver found him.

During that tour we came within an hour's drive of Auschwitz, the German Concentration Camp. I was always fascinated by history and thought it would be a wasted opportunity not to go and see the place whilst I was there. A very nice Polish lady offered to drive me there but it would mean getting up at some crazy early hour and rushing back to get on the bus for the next show. When that proposition was put to us, I accepted and everyone else declined. I'm glad I went to Auschwitz. You couldn't describe it as a pleasurable trip because of the nature of what was there but it is something special to see and experience a place rather than just read about it.

Walking around Auschwitz is a very sobering experience. Every single item that you see was used by one group of people to torture or kill another group. I think it's right that the place is open to the public as it can be easy for young people to forget just how horrible human beings can be to each other. Lots of people walking around were continually crying. It didn't affect me that way. I ended up in a sort of stupor. Perhaps the most awful sight there was a room full of children's shoes. There can be a tendency to put all of that horror into a box, shut the lid, and assert that it is all in the past now and won't ever happen again. For me there are two significant points here. Firstly, of course it can happen again. There always have been and always will be cruel tyrants in the world. Secondly, the negative spiritual force or energy from

which Auschwitz arose is alive and well and can be found in every human being at some point. There will never be any room for complacency in this regard.

By the end of the Polish tour, the singer Mike Munroe had decided to leave Hanoi Rocks. This would mean starting a completely new band but we were all ready for that challenge. There are some bootleg copies of the music on that tour. When we did the last concert, which was to be Mike's last ever with Hanoi Rocks, I had to smile as we played one of the band's biggest ever hits, 'Don't you ever leave me'!

By the end of that tour, it was also clear that Rene didn't really fit in. He always seemed to be incredibly stressed despite his gift for humour. Rene was like so many rock musicians – he always seemed to be just on the edge of big success but never actually got there. He died in 2003. It wasn't the typical overdose/hanging/car crash for him – those close to him feel that he died from a broken heart because he could never consummate his love affair with Rock'n'Roll.

Rene is a good example of how fame can be an extremely cruel mistress – the more you desire fame the more it will eat you up and spit you out. However, if you walk away from it, which I have done several times, it comes running after you to try and entice you back. I see a strange parallel here with gambling. When the gambler is desperate for one more win, he never wins. Whereas the beginner, who is just flirting with gambling with no real concern for the outcome, will often score.

I was lecturing in Las Vegas recently (more about that later) and I expounded my theory that you win if you don't care and you lose if you desperately want to win. That day in the casino a woman collapsed and was carried off in an ambulance. She had been sitting at the one-arm bandits for 30 hours straight. Before bed, I was challenged by one of the seminar attendees to bet one dollar before retiring, saying, "You're in Las Vegas, you have to gamble once!" I agreed and put one dollar into a slot machine. I didn't expect to win, I didn't care if I won, I was just going to go to bed. With one pull of the lever I won 36 dollars and promptly went to bed. My friends said, "Surely you're going to carry on now that you're on a winning streak?" I tried

to explain that the whole reason why I had won was that I didn't care and I was happy to walk away with the net increase of 35 dollars. As soon as you reinvest some of that 35 dollars you start to care whether you win and then you start to lose. Lots of people lust after fame – you can see it in so many reality TV shows. Others lust after money, perhaps a lottery win. It's so easy to waste your life wanting something you can't have rather than appreciating what you do have.

CHERRYBOMZ

Upon our return from Poland, we set about forming a new band with a nucleus of Andy McCoy, Nasty Suicide and myself. We needed a bass player and a singer. Timo had been Hanoi's roadie for a long time and people often remarked that he looked like he should be a member of the band and so we decided to give him a chance as the bass player – after all, it had worked well with Paul Simonon in The Clash (on the principle that it's better to find the right person and teach them to play bass rather than recruit the wrong person who happens to be able to play).

Andy called up a lady he had met called Anita Chellamah, Anita had trained as a dancer working with Legs & Co who used to perform on the TV show, *Top of the Pops*. She had also sung with Toto Coelo – who had a number one hit with the song, 'I eat cannibals'. With Anita on board we just needed a new name and a bunch of new songs. We called ourselves Cherrybomz. We inherited quite a few followers from the Hanoi fans and played numerous packed houses at the legendery Marquee Club in London. We then set off on a USA tour. At some point, Dave Tregunna came in on bass. He had worked with Sham 69 and would go on to form the Lords of the New Church with Stiv Bators. Stiv is no longer with us. He died (some say was murdered) in a hit and run in 1990.

In 1984 I was walking down the street in New York with Stiv and noticed a Rastafarian guy trying to sell drugs. He kept repeating, "Loose

joints, loose joints." Stiv said to him, "Well, you'd better see a chiropractor then." I had never heard the word chiropractor before, so I asked Stiv what it was. He replied, "Someone who fixes joints." Then his joke made sense. Funny how these seeds get planted when you least expect it.

Shortly before my 30th birthday I was touring with Cherrybomz across the USA. The manager called me up with an idea for a publicity stunt. The idea was to get a model from *Playboy*, or some other girly magazine, to pose naked all over my drum kit. I didn't like that idea at all so I told him to forget the whole thing, as it seemed cheap and tasteless. Sometimes in the music business when you say no they go ahead and do it anyway. This was something I was always wary of. When my 30th birthday came, I walked onto the stage at the theatre we were due to play that night. As I approached the drum riser, a mini-stage for the drumkit, I noticed from far off that there were flowers, champagne and balloons all over it. I immediately thought that they'd ignored my decision and gone ahead with this photo shoot idea. I flew into a rage, telling the road crew, "You can get this lot out of here right now!" Everyone's mouth dropped. No sooner did I finish the sentence when I noticed there were birthday cards amongst the balloons: It dawned on me that the display was nothing to do with the Playboy model but simply there to celebrate my birthday. I immediately changed my tone and turned to the shocked bystanders saying, "Only joking!" They all breathed a sigh of relief, laughed and said, "You really had us going there!" Just think how embarrassed I would have been if I hadn't noticed those birthday cards just in time.

After a year of extensive touring and recording the band split up. It felt a bit like The Clash break up in that we were all pushed a bit too hard. Anita and I have been close friends ever since. It did, however, get me started on doing drum solos.

Only a fool thinks that he has it all covered and doesn't need to improve. I fell into that trap in the eighties. I was playing to large audiences and I was also playing at a lot of drum clinics. This is where a well-known drummer performs for an audience of other drummers, showing them techniques, answering questions and explaining how to improve. I felt good about this

since it's a hundred times harder to impress an audience of fellow drummers than it is to impress an audience of rock fans. I had fallen into the trap of thinking I knew it all. The realisation came quickly. Here is how it happened.

Motley Crue were playing in London. Tommy Lee was the drummer. He had a great reputation as a live performer, so I arranged to go down and check them out. I met Tommy before the show and he seemed like a nice guy, although it's difficult not to hate a man who's married to Pamela Anderson. I sat back to watch the show, not dreaming for a minute that he would surprise me in any way. When it came to the drum solo, there was an atmosphere of excitement and expectation from the audience as the other band members walked off the stage. He astounded me (but nobody else!) by playing a simple drum pattern incredibly slowly. He asked the audience through his headset mike, "Do you want it faster?" I said to myself, "If he goes any slower he'll be going backwards!" The audience reacted with great enthusiasm and yelled for more. He slowly speeded up, each time asking the audience the same question. By the time he reached a respectable speed the audience was ecstatic. After that the whole drum riser turned upside down while he carried on playing. Both he and the drums were somehow strapped in. The painful part for me was that by now the audience were cheering much louder than they ever did for my solos. A friend who was with me put it very cleverly; "I realise that you can play faster and cleverer drum patterns than this guy. There are probably about a dozen other people here tonight who also realise that. There are 10,000 others who think he's much better than you." Words can never hurt you so much as when they are true.

I went to bed with my delicate ego thoroughly bruised, but I woke up with a great idea. If he can get such great reactions by using a bit of showmanship then why shouldn't I? I decided to make some drastic changes to my stage act. I decided that rather than trying to appeal to other drummers (0.1% of the audience) I would aim at impressing the rock fans (99.9% of the audience). My drum solo would start with some interesting sounds and rhythms; I would introduce some electronic effects to surprise people. I brought in Latin style percussion, the sort of thing you might hear on

the beach in Brazil. Then I would move into some very heavy Afro rhythms using large tom-toms and two bass drums. This would make the floor shake and get people in the crowd dancing and wiggling their hips. Then I would move into a close snare drum roll, the kind you might hear at a circus when acrobats are balancing 100 feet above ground. The lights would change at this point and build the tension until the final onslaught occurred. I would unleash everything I had at a furious speed, thrashing every drum and cymbal in sight. There would be massive echoes coming in and we would use strobe lighting so that it looked to the crowd as though I had at least four arms. This stuff would not go down well at a drum clinic but it always got me a standing ovation from a rock audience. Just because you are doing well doesn't mean that you can't do it better.

In 1985 Billy Idol asked me to come out to New York to work on his new album, which they had already recorded with a drum machine. They wanted me to put the drums on last with more feel than the drum machine. Unfortunately this really is the wrong way around. The only way to do it is to record the drums first with feel and have the other instruments play along. After a few days of bashing away in vain I suggested we start again from scratch but the prevailing view from Billy and Keith Forsey, the producer, was that they had gone too far and spent too much money to start again from scratch. That journey to New York turned out to be a waste of time although bizarrely I actually bumped into Joe Strummer in a bar and we had a good time catching up.

BLACK SABBATH

After the break up of the CherryBombz, I needed to find another band. I got a call out of the blue from Richard Bishop, my then manager, saying that Black Sabbath needed a drummer and was I interested? I had listened to Sabbath as a teenager and regarded them as the fathers of what is now commonly known as Heavy Metal. In particular, Tony Iommi was one

of the most influential guitar players in rock. I was excited at the prospect of working with them – it would give me the chance to go absolutely bonkers with big drum kits and drum solos in front of audiences who loved that type of thing. Having decided that this was the right step for me and I had to make sure that I would be the next drummer in Black Sabbath. This brings me to the subject of auditions.

When I worked with Billy Idol and Generation X we had to audition a new guitarist. I think we must have auditioned every guitarist in the Northern hemisphere. As a person who always approaches any project with huge enthusiasm and careful preparation, the high proportion of those guitarists who showed no enthusiasm amazed me. Nor had they done any preparation. When asked, "Do you want to be successful?" very few will say no. However, very few will exhibit behaviour that says yes. When I heard that Black Sabbath needed a new drummer I asked my manager to get in touch with them. The reply came back, "Yes, we'd like you to come down and audition with us and here are the names of three of our songs that we'd like you to learn in preparation." Now I really wanted that job. Firstly, this was a band that I had listened to as a teenager and really liked. Secondly, it was a rare opportunity to join a huge band that had then sold about 50 million albums. So the sensible, professional thing to do would have been to learn those three songs. But as well as that, I decided to apply massive enthusiasm.

I got hold of their live album and learned all the songs on that. I also learned the studio versions of the same songs, just in case. When I went along to play with the band, they asked me if I'd learned those three songs. They'd probably had the same experience as I'd had, of people coming along without the necessary enthusiasm. I replied that yes I knew the three songs and did they want me to play the studio or the live versions of them. After I'd played those three songs they asked whether I happened to know any others, to which I replied that I knew all the songs on the live album. You see, I knew how it felt to audition someone who hadn't bothered to learn the stuff and I wanted to make sure of getting this job by giving these guys the opposite feeling. The idea that someone knows the stuff already and you haven't got

to sit down and teach them always makes the band members really happy. After a few other songs, the band's leader, Tony Iommi, took me to one side and asked me if I really wanted to play in this band. "Yes," I said, "I most certainly do." He then went out and told the manager to cancel all of the other drummers who were due to audition. If there's something you really want I recommend this method of applying massive enthusiasm. It will take you a long way.

My first gig with Black Sabbath was to be Sun City, South Africa, in 1987. This was quite controversial at the time and proved to be a real eye-opener for me. There was lots of pressure in the music business and in other fields such as sport, to completely boycott South Africa, in an attempt to put pressure on them to end the Apartheid system. Some people were of the opinion that this was the opposite of what needed to be done. Such people would say that to go there and to engage with the South Africans is the only way to drag them into the 20th Century and a complete boycott would stop that happening. Paul Simon had gone there a year before and found some black South African musicians to work with. The result of that was the album, Gracelands, which was a big hit. At the time, I was stunned by the vicious criticism that Paul Simon had to endure when all he had done was to take some talented musicians and give them a chance to enhance their careers.

Black Sabbath also received some abuse. I read a newspaper article accusing Black Sabbath of playing to an all-white audience at Sun City. I talked to the journalist concerned and told him that not only was the audience of mixed races, but the place was also actually run by a black man. Rather than apologising for lying in his article, his answer was, "You shouldn't have gone there and you have to suffer the consequences." In other words he felt that because Apartheid was wrong, anyone who went to the country was wrong. Therefore any criticism of such people was justified, even if it were not true. I was shocked at the time but I have later come to realise that you have to be very careful around what I call anti-people. People who are anti-this or anti-that are remarkably similar to the people they are criticising. My view is that if the cause you are championing is based on hatred and involves lies, then

you are on the wrong track. Years later I read a quote from Mother Theresa who very wisely said, "I won't join an anti-war movement, but I will join a peace movement." Clearly she too had met her share of anti-people.

Talking of Africa, about 26 years ago, whilst travelling through the Sahara desert, I was bitten by a lion. I managed to survive. When I tell people that story they are shocked and start looking for the scars, missing limbs, etc. It is only later that I tell them that the lion was about eight weeks old. Somebody put the lion on my lap to pose for a photograph and it bit my thumb. I shrieked, as it really hurt. My friends all laughed, telling me it was only a little cub, so I invited them to put their hands in its mouth and tell me what they thought. Its jaws were larger than a pit bull terrier's.

My first public performance with Black Sabbath soon arrived. I was to meet the band downstairs in the hotel lobby in about half an hour. I was totally prepared, had rehearsed hard and knew exactly what to do. There is always some trepidation with a first ever performance. I knew that the audience would include management, record company people, journalists and die-hard fans, all of whom would expect a knock-out performance. However, there was a problem. A week earlier I had been to the dentist to have a new bridge fitted. At that time I was very vain, so I told the dentist to fit the bridge in a temporary way, and after I was satisfied that it looked and felt just right we would fix it permanently in place. The dentist agreed and after a couple of days I went back and told him yes, I was satisfied with it and he could fix it in my mouth permanently. The problem was that the temporary glue had stuck so hard that it just wouldn't come out. The dentist hammered away for a long time with all sorts of gadgets but it just wouldn't move. With some relief, I heard the dentist say, "If I can't get that bridge out with all this equipment, then it will never come out, so let's just leave it where it is."

With half an hour to spare before my performance, I decided to floss my teeth. To my utter horror . bridge not only came out but bounced on the sink and hit the stone floor, smashing to pieces. On this occasion I managed to focus on the solution rather than the problem. There was a pharmacy button on my hotel room telephone. I rang the pharmacist and

explained the problem. She said she would be there in ten minutes. She came in with a bag containing all sorts of bottles. I had managed to find all the pieces of ceramic material that made up the outer part of the bridge. She took a tube of super glue and glued them all back in place, just like a jigsaw. She then produced a tube of cement with which we fixed it back into my mouth. I managed to arrive on time and put on a performance that didn't disappoint anybody. It is amazing how often these mini-disasters happen just before you perform. How often in our lives do we exclaim, "Of all times for this to happen?" Perhaps upsets have to happen at a bad time if they are really going to teach you anything.

That first performance on stage with Black Sabbath was an interesting occasion. Here I was in a foreign country playing different songs, with a different band, in a different style, with a different mix of sounds on the stage, and added to all of that there was the drama with my tooth bridge just minutes before. Despite all this I was determined to keep my head clear of any distractions and have the highest possible level of present-time consciousness. Halfway through the first song it felt good. I could hear all the instruments, I was feeling comfortable and it seemed this was going to be a good performance. Then Tony Iommi, the guitar legend, turned around to look at me, pulling the most ridiculous face and balancing a pink guitar plectrum (pick) on the end of his nose. The thought occurred to me that out of all the thousands of people in the room, I was the only one who could actually see this. This was a peculiar thing to do but it made me feel good. It was a reminder that, with thousands of watts of sound and lights and a huge audience full of excitement, we could still enjoy some down to earth humour.

After finishing my first show with Black Sabbath we were getting changed when something odd happened. Tony Iommi amazed me as he calmly removed the tips of his fingers, put them into a box and packed it away. I learned that he'd had an accident as a young man, in which a machine in a sheet metal factory sliced off the tips of two fingers of his right hand. He thought his playing days were over until he found out that gypsy guitarist Django Reinhardt had lost the use of two fingers and still managed to become

a virtuoso musician. There is probably not a rock guitarist in the world that has not been influenced on some level by Tony Iommi. He later assured me that the rest of his body was original and authentic.

Sun City is a playground full of leisure pursuits. Since we were stuck there for about two weeks I saw all the shows and tried all the rides, but the thing I liked most was the ten-pin bowling, which I had never played before. I foolishly got the heaviest ball I could find and threw it down those lanes as hard as I could in order to better the score of my opponents. After three hours of this I discovered to my alarm that I had damaged my shoulder and I was quite unable to raise my arm. This might be okay if you were a singer but was a disaster for a drummer. I told Tony Iommi who seemed to be very nonchalant about it. He said, "No problem – we'll get a chiropractor in." I asked what this person was going to do and Tony said, "He'll fix you, of course."

Sure enough the chiropractor arrived and examined my shoulder and neck and then started treating me. He cracked my neck, which made an incredibly loud sound in my head, so loud that I thought he'd broken my neck. Before I could even consider the implications he cracked the other side. I thought to myself, "He's done it again!" But just as I was thinking this I realised I could now move my neck and my arm and I actually felt marvellous. I was instantly able to move my shoulder through its full range. I performed that night and was very grateful to the chiropractor whose name, regrettably, I cannot now call to mind. Hopefully he is still somewhere in South Africa saving rock drummers from disaster. I did not at that point leap up and decide to have an immediate career change but it did plant a further seed that was to germinate over the next year or so. Looking back on these little signposts on the way, I can't help feeling that a clear path was mapped out for me from the beginning.

After Sun City, the band went off on tour around Europe. Obviously I met a huge number of Black Sabbath fans who were an interesting bunch. Lots of them would say something like, "You've played with the boys but now you're playing with the men." It seems rock fans are a bit like football fans, whose loyalty is to the team regardless of who is playing in it. We were due

to play in a theatre in Rome. The Pope himself had been hosting an event in that theatre the night before. For some reason, they were unable to remove some of the equipment the Pope had been using in time for us to put our equipment in there. However big a band you are, you can't pull rank on the Pope in Rome! The promoter said that it wouldn't be a problem as they had another theatre they could shift our concert to.

What they didn't tell us was that there were 2,000 fewer seats in the new venue. The concert had sold out, which meant there were 2,000 people outside who had purchased a ticked but were denied entry. The crowd was not impressed. The ticket holders were told, "You can't come in. There is no room." To which they replied, "But I have a ticket." "Yes, you have a ticket but it is full up," was the response. A riot ensued, lots of local shops were smashed up and one person was shot (but fortunately not killed). We had two generators outside, one for the sound and one for the lights. The angry crowd proceeded to wreck one of the generators. We were given a stark choice – you can have either sound or lights but not both. A concert without any sound would be utterly ridiculous so we chose sound without light. We performed an entire concert in the dark with five roadies each with a torch shining on one of our faces. Actually the audience, those able to gain entry at least, seemed to really enjoy it!

When you put on a show it is usual to have a dress rehearsal. The dress rehearsal is a performance as near as possible to the exact conditions under which the real performance happens. There are very good reasons for doing this. I have rehearsed a song with a band until we have it perfect. We have then performed it on stage, where, because of the lights shining in our eyes, we've not been able to see each other properly and the nods and winks that we relied upon during rehearsals were simply not visible. The result is a poor performance. The dress rehearsal should take care of these unexpected problems, solving them before exposure to your audience.

A friend of mine called Russell was very interested in making costumes. He used to make his own fancy dress outfits that were unbelievably ambitious and achieved with great craftsmanship. Russell offered to make me an outfit

to wear onstage for the upcoming European tour. I accepted his offer and he produced an amazing garment for me to wear — a leather sleeveless jacket with incredibly intricate metalwork embedded in the leather. I decided to wear it at my next concert with Black Sabbath. However, I made the mistake of not having a dress rehearsal.

The first number we played that night was the longest song I can ever remember playing. In fact it lasted only three minutes. It seemed like a long time because, as I was vigorously thrashing those drums, my arms were moving up and down in a rapid sequence, as per normal. The problem was that the garment was lined with an extremely rough material. When the song ended, I yelled to the roadie to give me some duct tape. He gave me the duct tape with a somewhat bewildered expression, as I was normally very calm on stage. I tore off two pieces and promptly slapped one on each of my nipples, which were feeling as if they had been sandpapered for the last three minutes. I learned the lesson well that you must have a thorough dress rehearsal before going on stage in front of people. I doubt very much whether your job will ever involve sandpapering your nipples. However, the principle of thorough preparation can be useful in any work situation.

Tony Iommi was always fond of Rottweilers. He had a great big one called Bolo, after the character in the Bruce Lee movie, *Enter the Dragon*. The dog was well named, as he was all muscle, just like the character in the movie. I had met Bolo many times and he seemed to be quite a peaceful dog, even though he looked like he could eat you alive! I drove over to Tony's house and the gates were shut so I parked outside and walked through the small gate. It would have been about a 25-yard walk to his front porch. As I started walking, Bolo appeared at the side of the house. I told myself that this was fine as I had met him before and dogs tend to remember those they have met.

As I carried on walking calmly and confidently towards the porch two other Rottweilers appeared by Bolo's side. Clearly, it was too late to go back so I carried on walking. After all, I reasoned, the postman must do this every day. All three dogs then started to growl, that deep growl that only big, angry dogs can manage. They also started to edge slowly towards me whilst growling. At

this point I was about seven yards from the porch and they were about 12 yards away. If I simply carried on walking they were going to get to me before I got into the house. I had visions of one dog biting each leg, with another one biting my arm with only my left arm to defend myself. I didn't much like that scenario. It had occurred to me that if I took the initiative and sprinted to the porch, I would definitely be able to reach there before them.

With very little time to ponder the choice I broke into a dash for the porch door. Immediately the three dogs went crazy – barking and hurtling towards me. At this point I suddenly found myself asking the question, "Will the porch door be open? Because if it's not, I am literally dog meat." I grabbed the door handle and found it open. To say I was relieved would be an understatement. I got into the porch and shut the door with about one second to spare. Then, just like a scene in a horror movie, all I could see were teeth and dog saliva on the other side of the glass. With a great sigh of relief, I rang the doorbell. There was no answer. I determined that even if I had to stay there for a week I was not going outside that door. Tony arrived five minutes later and cheerfully said, "Oh! They won't hurt you!"

"No, of course not," I thought to myself...

I remembered again that old saying, "Only the good die young!"

It had been a real privilege to tour the world with a band I had admired as a kid. Furthermore, Black Sabbath at that time had realised that if you were going to tour you had to ditch the drugs and the drink and get the job done properly. As such they were perfectly in sync with what I wanted to do at that time. I remember the five of us entering a bar together. I walked up to the barman to order a round of drinks. He said, "I know who you guys are and I'm ready for anything – what can I get you?" I said, "Five Perriers please." His face dropped. He was sure I was joking, but that's what we wanted.

In 1998 I heard the news that yet another drummer had died – Cozy Powell, who was then playing in Black Sabbath. He crashed his car at 104 mph without wearing a seatbelt whilst being over the limit for alcohol and talking to his girlfriend on his mobile phone. It seems he hadn't adopted the Five Perriers approach.

It would have been entirely possible at that time just to carry on playing drums for various well-known bands and have a lucrative and interesting career. In fact that is what most musicians would have done at that stage. However, I felt the part of me that needed to heal people was wanting to have his turn in my life and the part of me that longed for just one more tour had by now been indulged enough. It was time for a change. There was one more thing that was starting to bother me – the death of so many of my drummer colleagues. It seems I was in the shortest-lived profession in the world…

CHAPTER 6
DEAD DRUMMERS DON'T LIE

These are my principles. If you don't like them, I have others.

Groucho Marx

Question: What do the following bands have in common?

- The Who
- Elton John band
- The Band
- Led Zeppelin
- The Beach Boys
- Fairport Convention
- The Carpenters
- The New York Dolls
- The Pink Fairies
- The Velvet Underground
- Hanoi Rocks
- The Ventures
- Echo & the Bunnymen
- Steely Dan
- Procol Harum
- Nazareth

- Rainbow

- Emerson, Lake & Powell

- Jefferson Airplane

- Devo

- Iron Maiden

- Lordi

- Rush

- Kiss

- Toto

Answer: In each of these, the drummer died first. In the cases of Rainbow and The New York Dolls, they had two drummers die! This may be of only passing interest to the average person, but when you're a drummer in a rock band, as I was for 15 years, it gets your attention. Even in the spoof film, *This is Spinal Tap*, the band went through a succession of drummers, one of whom spontaneously explodes. A simple internet search for dead drummers will reveal that the average life expectancy of a rock drummer is about 35 years, the most common causes of death being car crashes, overdoses and hanging. I decided early on that the traditional rock lifestyle combined with a likely early death was not for me. It was time for a change. Not a small change, such as moving from a punk band to a heavy metal band. Rather a profound leap with both feet into an entirely new field. Dr. Terry had been growing in me for 30 years and was about to wrest control from Mr Chimes. This was going to be a challenging but interesting journey. Before that, however…

NEAR DEATH EXPERIENCE NUMBER 3

I was in a band with my brother Bryn called Blood Simple. We were friends with a group of Hell's Angels who invited us to play at a big festival called The Bulldog Bash. After we played we spent some time watching a

couple of other bands from the side of the stage, then left. We had barely left the site when there was a newsflash on the radio. The stage at The Bulldog Bash was burning down. We were certain they were wrong as we'd only just left and everything was fine. We later heard that the guy frying chips near the side of the stage had decided to pour in some more cooking oil. He poured what he thought was a canister of oil, but it contained petrol. Anyone near that fryer was killed instantly. Bryn and I had been standing there for ages. What a shock that would have been for my mother!

IT ONLY FEELS KINKY THE FIRST TIME

Lots of people are terrified by the very thought of change – I see that all the time in patients who are stressed. Personally, I have always found change exhilarating. One of the reasons that change is so scary for some is the idea of being out of your comfort zone. I have found that you never know when you will be pulled out of your comfort zone – it happened to me quite recently. I was asked to be a judge at a dance contest. I have done this many times before and found it no problem. Usually the worst thing that can happen is that you are called upon to make a short speech and award a prize to the winner, which is not difficult if you have done that kind of thing before. This event was a Bollywood dance contest at a summer festival in the park.

I turned up and did my judging and as I gave out the prizes, along with several other judges, I felt that my job was done. At that moment, the host said, "if anyone would like to get up and try this Bollywood dancing for the first time they can come onto the stage now and try it!" As 30 or so people stepped up onto the stage, she said, to my dismay, "The judges can join in too". Now, I am not a dancer although, having played drums, I can at least manage to keep in time. They taught us a few Bollywood moves that we all did together. I made sure I stayed near the back. They then picked out three judges from the audience to assess the group on the stage. When they asked the judges for a verdict, they conferred and then pronounced that the winners were, "This eight year old girl and him."

You can imagine my horror when I realised that him was me! Everyone else left the stage in preparation for me to compete with the eight-year-old girl for the prize. I know that there was no risk of death in all of this, but nevertheless, to perform a Bollywood dance for the first time, in front of several thousand Indians, most of whom know how it should be done, was just a little beyond my usual comfort zone. I went through the whole routine with the eight year old whereupon the judges were asked to award the first prize. Just when I thought things couldn't get any worse, the judges were unable to agree on the winner and asked us to perform one more time. All I could think was, "She is a child, for God's sake, give her the prize and get me out of here!" Finally they gave the young girl the first prize and I scurried off out of sight. I saw the Mayor on the way out, who was one of the other judges and told him I was going to demand an enquiry as to why I hadn't won. More seriously, I feel strongly that those who never dare to get out of their comfort zone are severely limited in life.

My change of career from being a rock musician to a chiropractor may seem like a large jump. It is perhaps the question I am most frequently asked when people meet me – how do you go from being one to the other? I include this story here, so that in future when people ask me that question, I can simply say, "It's all in the book."

It was never my intention to spend my whole life as a musician. The life of an artist can be tough, and if you are going to do it, it is best done when you are young. Life as a rock musician consists of a never-ending cycle of travelling from town to town, and going to parties every night. When you are 19 years old, this is fine, but the appeal wears off over the years. Conversely, most people don't like to see a very young doctor, on the basis that they are too young to know anything yet. My father had been a musician but did not pursue a professional music career since the demands of a young family required stable employment. For that reason I feel he was very gratified to see all three of his sons go on to become professional musicians. However, even as a small child, I felt a strong pull towards medicine. As a teenager I was still interested in medicine, but by then I had discovered girls...

It seemed to me that there were two ways to get the girls. One was to be a football player; the other was to be a rock musician. Since I was useless at sport, there was really only one choice open to me. I thoroughly enjoyed my fifteen years as a professional musician, and I would not have wanted it any other way. However, the urge to treat my ailing fellow human beings was steadily growing stronger. Since I was already into my thirties, I decided that such a big change should happen sooner rather than later, as the large amount of studying involved was likely to be harder as I got older. In the circumstances, it wasn't possible for me to effect the change gradually. It was necessary to jump in with both feet. If you spend years working your way up in any profession and have reached a certain level of respect from your peers, as well as a satisfactory income, it can be very difficult to start again at the bottom in another field. I dismissed this concern early on, as I reasoned that I would only be at the bottom for a relatively short time, and this was a career for the rest of my life so it would be well worth the initial sacrifices. Also, since I had never been to university, I was excited by the prospect of learning and broadening my mind on a full-time basis. I have always thought that further education is a great privilege and sometimes not appreciated by the very young. I relished the prospect of spending years delving into books, experimenting in the laboratory and engaging with learned people on the very topics that had always fascinated me.

The question I am very often asked is "How could you give up stardom for treating sick people?" I will try to explain this as best I can so you can see what makes healing is so irresistible.

When we played the Olympic Stadium in Los Angeles there were 100,000 people in the audience. I remember thinking before going onstage that I had to enjoy this experience, because I might not play to such a large audience ever again. If you had told me at the age of sixteen that I would be on TV, have number one hits and play to such large audiences, I would have been absolutely ecstatic. The truth is that when I did all that, while I was generally happy, I was not ecstatic, and the expected euphoria just wasn't there. I am not saying that I didn't enjoy my music career, and I most certainly

would do it all over again, but years later I found myself standing in front of a 12-year-old boy who had, throughout his life, woken up every morning soaked in his own urine. After three weeks of treatment, he reported to me that for the last five mornings he had woken up completely dry. The boy was quite nonchalant about this, but his mother was unable to hold back the tears. The problem that had blighted his entire life was now solved. There were not 100,000 people in that room, only the boy and his mother. The feeling I got from having changed that boy's life was the euphoric feeling that I had been searching for all these years.

Making such a difference to the lives of others has given me a much more profound happiness than I ever managed on the stage. It is a case of doing what you love and loving what you do. My clinics have so far seen 44,000 patients; so it's just possible that I will ultimately reach 100,000 people, but one at a time. How many people out there are just one step away from profound happiness but are just too scared to get out of their comfort zone by taking that step outside it? In my practice I've seen too many people who are so scared of change that they stay for years in a place they'd rather not be. Just one proviso; you can change your politics, your religion, your appearance, and even your sex! But you must never change the football team you support. Up the Hammers!

———•———

Around the time I decided to enrol on a course in medical sciences I found the ideal course run by an osteopath called Joe Goodman. The fee for the first year of that course was £1,000. The mortgage interest rate had just gone through the roof (to around 15%) leaving me broke, albeit with a nice house. I didn't have £1,000 but I enrolled anyway, thinking I would find it from somewhere. A week before the payment was due we had a family dinner at which my father stood up unexpectedly and made a little speech. It seemed my parents had been putting away a little money each month into a savings scheme and it had just borne fruit. My father told us how proud he was of all of us, not so much because of what we had achieved, but because of how we

had all turned out. He then gave each of us a cheque for £1,000. My parents had no idea at that time that I needed that very sum. I don't know what my two brothers did with theirs but for me it was an unbelievable coincidence that the exact amount of money came at exactly the right time. This was a further indication to me that there was a guiding hand exerting a benevolent influence over my life, more noticeable at times like these.

When I was interviewed for a place at chiropractic school in Bournemouth, I was struck by the difference between that interview and my previous interviews at medical school. They asked me why I wanted to be a chiropractor and told me that before being allowed on the course I would have to pass a further interview by the Chiropractic Association. This interview would be by a practitioner in the field who was going to make sure I was the right type of person to join the profession. I was interviewed by a Dr Starkey (curiously reminding me of Ringo's real name). He was a very pleasant man who spent a good deal of time with me in an effort to discover if I was an appropriate person to join his profession. Looking back, this seemed like a really good idea because in my twenty years of healing people I have met quite a few doctors and therapists who really should be doing something else. I jumped that hurdle and signed up to spend the next four years of my life in full-time study.

When I was leaving home to go and study in Bournemouth, an old friend called Angie Arnold commented that the people I would meet the next day would be the people I would be very close to for the duration of the course and some of them would probably become life-long friends. I turned up at Bournemouth with that thought in mind. I was going to study full time for four years and would have virtually no concerns other than filling my head with lots of useful knowledge. Some 18 year olds might well take this for granted but it seemed like a big privilege to me.

I arrived late and sat down next to a very gentlemanly chap who was about 12 years older than me – his name was Paul Brindley. I asked him if I had missed anything important in the last couple of hours. He reassured me in a very convincing way that I had missed nothing of any importance. I

spent the next four years sitting next to Paul during which time he gave me numerous such assurances. When I first arrived at College, I didn't tell people about my musical past. I had finally taken up my calling to the healing arts. I was here to learn and didn't want the distraction of others making a fuss of my past. However, keeping my past a secret turned out to be futile. I had been at the college for about a year when they used the song, 'Should I Stay or Should I Go?' in a Levi's jeans commercial, Joe Strummer and I having long ago agreed that Levi's were the best jeans. The song immediately went to number one in the charts and stayed there for several weeks. The video was played endlessly on TV at that time and the striking resemblance between the guy in the video and myself was impossible to miss. People thought it even weirder that I hadn't said anything so I might as well have told them in the first place. Not for the first time in my life, I discovered that honesty really is the best policy.

I had a great time being a student. It was a bit like being in a band but with less money. By that, I mean that the rest of the world was out there working whilst you had jumped off the merry-go-round to do something else for a while.

During the first year at chiropractic school it was obvious to me that studying in groups was more effective for several reasons. I teamed up with a fellow mature student called Sean Moruzzi. Various people joined and left the study group over the years but Sean and I were always there. He would turn up with six textbooks and four folders of notes whereas I would have everything summarised on a small piece of paper. He would say it made him nervous not to have every piece of information possible whereas I would be nervous if I couldn't fit the whole topic onto a scrap of paper. Sean and I made a pact; we would make sure that neither of us failed a single exam. Happily, we succeeded.

Some people are really not cut out for anything medical and will pass out at the mere mention of blood, never mind the sight of it. Such people are appalled by the idea of dissecting the human body and find it particularly odd that someone like me, as a vegetarian, could stand such a thing. I have often

pointed out that I am only dissecting, not eating these bodies. Actually, you are so busy figuring out which muscles and nerves are which, you don't have time to worry about who they are. You are very grateful that they have donated their body but you're too busy trying to pass exams to think much further than that. Furthermore, these things are essential to gain your qualifications but you are never going to have to do them again after graduating.

Even as a full-time student my entrepreneurial spirit was still alive and kicking. Every term the professors would give us a list of books that we had to buy. Some of these were very expensive because they were so specialised. I opened accounts with all of the major book publishers and bought enough copies of each of the required books for about half of the class. As I had no overheads, I was able to sell the books at a discounted price and make a good profit, and I always sold every copy. Being a full time student gets expensive and this helped me pay my way.

I had always suffered from hay fever but not badly enough to bother with medication. In the summer of my first year at chiropractic school I went home and cut my hedge, which was about 150 feet long. The hedge was in flower and, as a result, I got hay fever from hell. I could hardly see because my eyes were itching like crazy, I had a pounding headache, my nose was running like a tap and, worst of all, my palate was so itchy I could have happily scrubbed it with a wire brush. Anyone who has suffered hay fever will recognise this pattern. As luck would have it my wife, Maxine, had just recently finished a course in acupuncture and seized upon the opportunity to use her new skills. I was suffering so badly I would have agreed to anything. She inserted about half a dozen needles. I was hoping for a slight reduction in my symptoms but within 20 minutes my headache had gone, my nose had not only stopped running but also completely dried up like a desert and all the itchiness in my eyes and palate had vanished. I decided right there and then that if acupuncture could control the nervous system in this way then I just had to learn it.

I went back to study at the age of 33 and I was concerned that perhaps my brain wouldn't be as sharp as it had been at 18. However, having completed

the first year of study and passed all the exams, I realised that I had the capacity to take on a bit more. I decided that I wanted to do acupuncture as well as chiropractic but I couldn't face doing one course and then the other consecutively because I reckoned I'd be 90 years old by the time I finished. I talked to the acupuncture college about doing the acupuncture degree at the same time as the chiropractic degree by working at weekends and evenings. They told me this wasn't really feasible and that I should make another plan. I insisted that it could be done and that I wanted the opportunity. They eventually allowed me to start the second degree but they reserved the right to terminate that arrangement with the first sign that I wasn't able to cover the work.

Acupuncture and chiropractic are both alternatives to drugs and surgery but have very little in common when it comes to the subject matter. So every time we breathed a huge sigh of relief when the chiropractic exams finished, I had to cram for two further weeks for the acupuncture exams. This went on for three more years.

Because of the large amount of material I had to memorise, I decided to find out if the super power memory books I had seen in bookshops were any good. I bought one and spent a whole weekend trying to improve my memory. This proved to be quite a revelation and taught me that people don't really have good or bad memories; they either use their memory or don't. If you learn to use your memory the power is incredible. Just for fun, I learned how to memorise the position of each card in a deck of cards. I would get someone to shuffle the pack and then I'd look at each card in turn, memorising its position from 1 to 52. After doing that the person would ask me either (a) what card is no. 32, to which I would reply the Jack of diamonds, or (b) where is the two of Clubs, and I would say no. 15. Whilst this impressed some of my friends and family at the time, it was a bad mistake. For years after, every time I forgot something they would point their finger at me and laugh, saying, "Memory man has forgotten something!" So while I recommend improving your memory I would resist the temptation to show-off.

Being a student was a bit more expensive than I had anticipated. In fact just about everything that I experience in life is more expensive than

anticipated! I needed some more income, as I didn't really want to borrow money. The obvious thing was to play some music and I found that Germany was the perfect place as they have an insatiable appetite for old English music. I flew over at weekends, which was a pleasant relief from all the studying, and I met various old friends whilst doing it, such as Dave Dee – sadly no longer with us, even though he wasn't a drummer!

Around the time that I completely changed my career I also separated from Maxine after eleven years. That might sound like a brief marriage but in the music business it's a marathon. She kept the home in Northampton and I stayed down in Bournemouth to further my studies. We didn't actually divorce for a long time, as there was nobody else involved. I am happy to say that Maxine and I have remained friends over the years. She later called me to say that Denis the dog was going crazy and ripping up all the furniture in the house, especially the mattresses. I think he missed me, as I was the one he'd bonded with. I collected him and took him to Bournemouth to live with me. On the first night in his new home he proceeded to rip up the furniture there too. Luckily the people I was sharing the flat with were dog-lovers and very understanding. He settled down after a few days, having cost me a fortune in mattresses.

I also filmed an instructional drum video to help young drummers improve. I got my brother Bryn to help me as he was always fascinated by the film industry. We wrote the script, hired all the equipment and camera crew, and aimed to record the whole thing over one weekend. At that point, I knew very little about project management and I hadn't planned what we were going to do about editing the video. Video-editing is a time-consuming and costly affair. But for the moment my only concern was to get the filming done. A guy walked in, during the filming and asked us if we would mind him watching for a while. To which we said, "No problem, as long as you don't make any noise whilst we're filming."

When the tea break finally came, he said to me, "You don't remember me, do you?" I apologised and admitted that I did not whereupon he explained that several years earlier his girlfriend had wanted to record her first single but didn't have the money to do it. Bryn, myself and a couple of pals had agreed to play the backing track for her at no cost, just to help her out. We did that

on the basis that if it were a hit we would get paid to do the album, and if it were a flop we would have lost nothing. Unfortunately, the record was not a hit, but this man had remembered that we had done him a favour, which he would now like to return. He worked in a video edit suite and told us that when we came to edit the video he would allow us to go in there either at night or at the weekend when it wasn't busy and let us edit our video for free. We accepted his kind offer and he did a great job with the edit. I have never been one to agree with the expression, "Nice guys finish last." My experience has usually been the reverse.

During my studies, I went to the wedding of my old manager Richard Bishop in Los Angeles. It gave me the chance to hook up with Hanoi Rocks guitarist, Andy McCoy, and his beautiful new wife, Angela. I was only there for a long weekend and I somehow ended up sharing an apartment with two models. I had one day free and the sun was shining. The girls told me they were going roller skating and invited me to come along. I politely refused since I have never been able to roller skate. They told me, "It's easy – we'll show you how". I tried to explain that I really couldn't do it but they insisted so I gave in and went to the beach with them. When we got the skates on and tried to skate they were genuinely shocked that I really could not skate, even though I had told them several times. They quickly came up with the solution, which was to hold one hand each and take me for a ride. I can distinctly remember the incredulous looks from various men obviously thinking, "What the hell is that guy doing with these gorgeous girls when he can't even skate?" The next day I went to a wonderful wedding at the Bel Air hotel and then flew back to carry on studying.

I got involved in the Student Union as the PR person. At the end of your year of office you have to make a short speech about what has been achieved. It just so happened that two major PR events occurred during my year. Firstly, the Medical Research Council published an article showing chiropractic to be better for lower back pain than hospital outpatient treatment, and secondly, Lady Diana announced that she was having great results with chiropractic. She became our patron and actually flew into the college by helicopter to

make a speech. PR for chiropractic that year increased 1,000%. This had nothing to do with my PR abilities; it was just a happy coincidence.

Years later, several of us asked around our colleagues to find out who was treating Lady Diana but nobody owned up to it. This of course is quite right according to our ethical code but normally one would expect such information to be shared between a few carefully chosen colleagues. I eventually found out years later that it was a good friend of mine and a great chiropractor called Graham Heale – tragically killed in a motorcycle accident a couple of years ago.

While I enjoyed being a student, in the final year I couldn't wait to escape. I had wanted to heal people from the age of 8 and was now on the verge of being unleashed upon the great British public. It's true that as a final year intern you are treating patients but you are in such a controlled environment that the experience is very frustrating.

The day eventually arrived for my final exam. This was the one that all students dreaded. We'd all seen students from earlier years trembling at the thought of it or rushing away in tears when they'd finished. It was a viva where three doctors sat there and asked questions. You couldn't really prepare for it because they could ask you just about anything. I was relatively calm about it for two reasons. Firstly, Sean and I had studied together for four years and we'd never had a failure yet. Secondly, I saw this as a performance and I'd been performing all my life. Still, I was looking forward to getting the other side of it. I went in feeling calm and reasonably confident.

They started asking me about whiplash injuries, which was fine. They moved on to nutrition – no problem there. They gave me some x-rays to read and I diagnosed the problem correctly. I was getting comfortable now. Then came the crunch – they asked a simple and apparently easy question. "How would smoking affect a back sufferer?" I shot straight back at them all the problems caused by lower oxygen levels and the resultant slower healing. They said, "Anything else?" Then I blasted them with decreased vitamin C absorption with the resulting poor quality of cartilage produced. I explained

all the metabolic pathways to back this up then sat back thinking I'd defeated them. Then they said. "Anything else?" I thought to myself, 'I've told them everything — what more could they possibly want?' I gave in and said no, I couldn't think of anything else. They took great pleasure in saying, "Do you think a smoker might cough more than the average person?" I'd been so carried away with the details that I couldn't see the wood for the trees. I did, however, pass the exam.

On the day that my final exam results came in I had already pre-arranged my insurance cover and professional association membership — I simply needed to hear the word that I had attained my degree. When I finally got the word, my first patient was in front of me within two hours. Bizarrely, I was half way through treating him when he asked the question, "How long have you been doing this for?" If I had replied, "You are my first patient" he would no doubt have laughed, thinking I was joking. I took the safer option and told him I had been treating patients for a year, which was true, as I had been treating patients in the student clinic for that time. I found it incredible that my very first patient asked that question. It was probably a year before anyone else asked it again.

My graduation ceremony in 1993 was a nice milestone for several reasons. Firstly, I had finally managed a complete transformation from rock musician to chiropractor — and that felt good. I had gone from the shortest-lived profession to reputedly the longest-lived profession in one jump. More importantly, I had made my parents happy. My mother no doubt frequently had nightmares about my death in a motorcycle accident or some other early rock death scenario. Years earlier, my brother John recounted to me the story of when I first started to ride motorbikes. My mum was horrified and said so to the rest of the family (I was out at the time). They tried to tell her that I would be OK but she was far from convinced. They decided to stop arguing and settle down to watch the evening movie on TV. The movie was *Lawrence of Arabia*, which begins with Lawrence riding along on a motorbike, crashing and dying. I think she was relieved to hear I had stopped riding motorbikes and thrilled to hear that I was going back to study.

I moved back to my parents' house in London and went to work in a nearby clinic housed in a very elegant, high-class building. No expense had been spared in the setting up. The clinic had recently opened and accommodated many different therapists. I arrived there with a clear idea of what I wanted, which was lots of patients. On my first day I walked into the quietist building in the world. I made some noise and a nice lady called Chris appeared, looking somewhat surprised. I told her I was the new chiropractor and the surprise left her. Chris was destined to be my head receptionist for the next 17 years. I was shocked to find that, despite the luxurious surroundings, there were hardly any patients. There were plenty of therapists, all sitting around doing nothing. My self-image as the busiest chiropractor in London was not matching the reality. One of these had to change, and I was damn sure which one it was going to be.

I needed to immediately find a way of generating patients for myself. I printed thousands of leaflets offering a free check-up. I had lots of young kids running around the local streets, putting the leaflets through doors. Like clockwork, the next day the phone would ring and lots of new patients would book in with me. I quickly built a large practice in this way but, of the 14 therapists at the clinic, I was the only one who was busy. Then my inner voice told me to find another building for my practice. I ignored this at first because there seemed to be no need, and it would have been disloyal to David, the man who had given me my first chance.

The voice became more and more insistent and was eventually impossible to ignore. Just to appease the voice and without any real intention of moving, I checked to see if there were any properties to rent. There was one right around the corner. It was in an ideal location and just the right size. I thought it couldn't hurt to look, so I went in. The owners occupied the upper floor and wanted to rent the ground floor. They were very friendly and helpful and loved the idea of a clinic downstairs. A bank that no longer needed it had leased the ground floor but had three years remaining on the lease, so they wanted to sublet it. I hit on a great idea to silence the voice. I would offer an insulting 50% of the rent and, just to make sure it was refused,

I also insisted on the first six months rent-free. I phoned my insulting offer through to the agent and went back to work feeling nice and calm. To my horror, they called back within the hour and accepted my offer! Then the battle between my heart and my head really started raging. The inner voice by now was shouting so loud that I just had to trust it and obey, so I instructed a lawyer, but told him to take plenty of time over it. I figured that lawyers take ages when you are rushing them so this was going to take forever. Anyway, if I signed the lease, I could always sublet to someone else.

A few weeks later, David came to me and told me he was shutting down, as he was making a loss. We had two weeks to get out. The inner voice had been right all along. I called the lawyer and said, "You know I told you to take your time?" "Yes," he replied. "Well now I need you to pull out all the stops and get me in there by the weekend!" That was just enough time to decorate part of the new building, divert the phone, re-install the x-ray machine, write to all the current patients, and about 10,000 other tasks. Two weeks later, I was in my own clinic, which is still there and is one of the busiest chiropractic clinics in Europe. Had I started to look for a place after David told me, it would have meant at least 6 weeks with nowhere to practice. The inner voice will seldom let you down, but sometimes it is necessary to trust it even when it doesn't seem to make any sense.

I then settled happily into a routine of working hard and getting people well. I got up early one very cold December morning. It had snowed the night before so I had to defrost the car before I drove off. I had a very quiet V12 Jaguar and I remember hearing the sound of those huge tyres crushing the virgin snow. It was such a beautiful morning and I had that 'great to be alive' feeling. Then I felt a hand rest on my shoulder. To say I was not expecting that is a major understatement. In the half second or so it took me to look around I replayed a dozen horror films featuring a mad axe-man in the back of the car. When I turned around it was not a mad axe-man. In fact, it was not even a human being. A cat had crept into the car while I was de-icing the screen and had decided to jump onto my shoulder. I stopped the car and opened the door. The cat ran out, looking back at me with an expression that implied, "I've had enough of you!" "I've had enough of you too!" I thought.

CHANGING MY WAYS

In 1998 I decided to throw a party. I put together a list of friends and called or e-mailed them, asking them to respond yes, no or maybe. In due course I checked their replies to see how many were coming so I could get in the right amount of food and drink. There were about 80 people who said yes, but I knew from previous experience that not all of them would show up. As I looked down the list of names, I began asking myself how reliable each person was. I came across the names of a couple called Gary and Laura. I have known these two for many years, and in all that time I have never been let down by them, not even once. As I looked at their names, I found myself smiling and thinking how nice it was that they were so reliable. I really liked the fact that they respected me so much that they never went back on their word to me. Not only that, I also knew that they would be on time. Why? Because they always were. They respected me enough not to waste my time. I just sat there and reflected on how nice it is to have friends whom you can rely on. I also reflected on how odd it was that I had never paid much attention to this in the past. Then I looked further down the list at some more names, many of whom I knew to be very unreliable. So if they said yes, I am definitely coming, I estimated perhaps a 50% likelihood of them actually showing up. When I had finished, I managed to make a fairly accurate guess as to the actual number of people I needed to cater for. What happened next was something I shall never forget.

I put the list to one side and then I started to wonder how reliable I was myself. As I thought back over many years, I realised that I had been far from reliable. I could remember many occasions when I had said, "Yes, I'll be there" and then didn't show up, usually because I didn't feel like it. In other words, my reasons were basically selfish. I also suspected that for each one that I remembered, there were many others long forgotten. People don't usually

call the next day and ask, "Where the hell were you?" No, they just let it go. I had never before asked the question, "Am I reliable?" Now I was asking it for the first time and I was dismayed at the answer: an emphatic no. I then played out in my head possible conversations between my friends and associates, going something like this. "Terry Chimes said he's coming tonight", then the answer, "Yeah, but you know what he's like, he only turns up if he feels in the mood, you could wait all night for him". This would be followed by general nods in agreement. What a horrible thought! The good part was that now I was finally paying attention to this, I realised that this was no bad dream; this sort of conversation (or worse) would definitely have taken place on many occasions. There was only one thing to do. I was going to have to change.

I started to imagine what it would be like to be utterly reliable, to know that when you said the words, "I will be there," the other person would be happy to know that you meant it. I was well aware that you could not acquire a reputation for being dependable overnight; that, of course, would take a long time. What I did know was that I could start being dependable right now, this moment. I enjoyed that powerful feeling of taking control of my life and making a change for the better. The trouble was that before I could really enjoy it, I started to think about another problem. I had not only been unreliable but I was often late as well. This was a separate, but not unrelated, problem. Both have a lot to do with how much respect you give to other people. Try as I might, I could not take any pleasure in being the new reliable me until I had fixed this second problem.

At first, I started to make excuses such as bad traffic and unreliable trains. Then I realised that I usually allowed just enough time for the journey, with no allowance for delays. Since there usually were delays, I was usually late. It was as simple as that. I made up my mind that I would aim to leave half an hour early (more on a very long journey) and always bring a book to read so as never to waste any of my time. Also, being early would ensure that I would not waste anybody else's time. I started feeling much better now, because even though I hadn't actually arrived early anywhere yet, I had made a life-changing decision, and that was sufficient for me to gently bathe in the

pleasant warm afterglow of pride that was spreading through the new me. Unfortunately, there was still a nagging doubt within me.

With growing concern that I had just created a monster that was never going to allow me to sleep again, I turned my attention to the next problem. I was in the habit of saying, "I will call you", "I will lend you that book" or "give you that website address." I would make these promises without any real commitment to carrying them out. It wasn't that I had no intention of delivering on these promises; I just had a tendency to not get around to it unless I received one or more reminders. This smacked of the same old problem yet again: not giving other people enough respect. I was really in the flow of making life-changing decisions now, so it was comparatively easy to make one more. Plus, I was desperate to get some sleep. I resolved that in the future, if Terry Chimes promises something to anyone, then he will do his utmost to deliver on that promise no matter what the cost in terms of time, money, energy or anything else. I did not intend to make fewer promises, just deliver on the ones that I did make. Finally, I felt the tension leave me so that the new Terry could feel the harmony returning and fall asleep, dreaming about this wonderful person he was going to become. The next day, I wrote down my promises to myself and started to act on them.

It was quite soon after the night of the birth of the new Terry that I had a chance to make good on a promise. My friend Sam Jacobs had phoned a month earlier to ask if I would like to join him and four other friends at a concert. I had said, "Yes please, get me a ticket". When the day arrived, as is so often the case, I was really not in the mood. I was very tired after a previous late night, but I had promised and this was an opportunity to show the world what the new me was like. So I not only showed up, but – you guessed it – I was half an hour early. When I arrived, I saw Sam approaching several people outside the theatre. He explained to me that three of the four others had called that afternoon to cancel, so he was trying, without success, to sell the tickets. Furthermore, the fourth person didn't show up either. As we walked in, Sam said to me, "I'm glad you showed up or I would be on my own." I was quite unable to resist the temptation to declare to Sam, "If

I promise to do something, I always make every effort not to let that person down." Sam looked at me with a somewhat surprised expression and said, "I really appreciate that." I felt good that I had not let him down and that it was appreciated, and right then I decided that the new me was here to stay.

When a man makes a promise, he creates an island of certainty in a heaving ocean of uncertainty. When you make a promise you have created a small sanctuary of trust within the jungle of unpredictability.

Lewis Smedes

The next week I tried something new. I had never been one to be late for work, but someone once said to me, "If you are on time, then you are half an hour late." This resonated with me at a deep level, so I resolved to arrive at my practice at least 30 minutes before the first patient. When I tried it the first time, I was surprised at not being the first in. My two receptionists were both there already. They had got into the habit of arriving early to check a whole list of jobs. Were the rooms warm enough? Did any patient gowns need washing? Was there enough change in the till? Plus a score of other items. They had learned long ago that it's much less stressful to be early and not get caught out. I then decided that it would be a good idea to briefly read each patient card so that I would familiarise myself with each case and mentally prepare to meet each person, as they all have a different story. This actually took up all of the 30 minutes, but was so useful, and made the work so much more efficient, that I have done it ever since.

Rock musicians are not known for being punctual. The first live gig I ever played with Black Sabbath, we had all been told to meet in the hotel lobby at 8 pm. At that stage I had been in the rock business for a long time and, in rock and roll language 8pm usually means some time before 9pm I went down there at ten minutes past eight which I thought was quite early and everyone was there waiting. It seems that when some people say 8pm, they actually mean 8pm. There were times with other bands when they would

phone your room and say "Please come downstairs, we're going," and each of the band members would ask, "Are the others there yet?"

There was a time when I wanted some publicity for a couple of projects that I was involved with. My friend George was an editor with the *Daily Star* newspaper. I asked him if I could do an interview to publicise my new projects. George arranged the interview, during which I told the journalist all about the projects. She asked me to talk about all the wild parties during my time in the rock business, and I replied that I didn't want to go into that territory. She asked me about my declaration that I don't drink, smoke or take drugs and whether I had ever drunk alcohol. I told her that I used to drink, like any other person, but I gave up in 1982. When the article was published it occupied a full page. There was no mention of any of the projects I wanted to publicise and the headline was 'Terry's battle with the booze'. My friends all thought it was hilarious. I called George to complain and he said he had been on holiday that week, otherwise it wouldn't have happened.

CHINA

After my graduation in 1993, I went to Nanjing, China to spend six weeks working in a hospital doing acupuncture on patients with all sorts of complaints. There are certainly plenty of people there to practice on. On the day I started I was shocked to see how fast they treated patients, but I was soon doing the same thing. We saw a vast range of conditions from morning sickness to migraines and from frozen shoulders to hot flushes. There was always an interpreter available but I soon learned that not being able to chat was not usually an obstacle. They certainly let you know if they were in pain and their smiles told you when they were getting better.

I was particularly impressed by the way the Chinese doctors integrated traditional Chinese medicine with modern western medicine. For instance, if a patient turned up having fallen on his arm, he would be sent to the orthopaedic ward for an x-ray to see if there was a fracture. If there was no

fracture he would be referred to the acupuncture department for pain relief. It's such a shame that we can't work together more often like that in the west.

Each morning there was a meeting between the head doctor and myself. An interpreter always joined us. One day I found myself sitting opposite the head doctor as usual, but there was no interpreter, who, it seemed, was sick. After waiting a few minutes, the doctor went off to make some inquiries. On her return, she amazed me by speaking in perfectly fluent English. I thought I was dreaming, as she had always spoken to me in Chinese, through the interpreter. When I spoke about this to some Chinese friends, they explained that for the doctor to speak English to me would embarrass the interpreter. Sure enough, as soon as the interpreter returned, she reverted to Chinese and only spoke English to me again when we said goodbye. If only we in the West were that sensitive to each other's feelings.

It's possible for acupuncturists to treat themselves although it's always better for someone else to treat you if possible. I was sitting at home with a sinus infection and there was nobody available to give me any treatment so I decided to treat myself. There are some acupuncture points that are very effective for sinus problems but it means inserting needles into points located on the face. This is nowhere near as painful as it sounds but it can look a bit strange to the uninitiated. I sat with these pins in my face watching TV and quite forgot they were there. There was a knock at the door and I answered, forgetting that these pins were still protruding from my face! To this day, I have no idea who the man was or what he wanted. He simply quickly made his excuses and rushed off! I imagine he still tells the story about the crazy man with pins in his face.

I've treated thousands of people and learned a lot about health and disease. I haven't the space here to tell you everything but I must take the opportunity to tell you how I got here and share some of my experiences.

*Terry and his
lethal weapon
by Jerry Green*

Above: Terry at a drum clinic by Maxine Chimes

Below: GenX: L-R James Stevenson, Billy Idol, Tony James, Terry

Above: Terry's first clinic *Below: One of 250,000 treatments*

Above: The Crunch: Terry, Sulo, Dave Tregunna, Mike Geggus by Luke Billing

Engraving on zinc by Terry's father

Above: Terry, Mick Jones and Joe Strummer's widow, Lucinda

Below: Terry Chimes, Mick Jones and Paul Simonon of The Clash

Photo by Dimitrios Kambouris

Left:
Terry Chimes,
Mick Jones and
Paul Simonon
of The Clash

Photo by Jim Spellman/WireImage

Below: The Edge of U2 with Terry Chimes, Mick Jones and
Paul Simonon of The Clash and Tom Morello of Audioslave

Photo by RJ Capak/WireImage

Portrait of Terry Chimes by Michael McGuinness (2009)

CHAPTER 7
THE JOURNEY OF THE
WOUNDED HEALER

Choose a job you love, and you will never have to work a day in your life.

Confucius

Those who pursue a career in the healing arts often do so after having been wounded themselves. It's as though they get healed and then want to do the same for others. I received my wound at the age of 15. I had some vaccinations for typhoid and cholera. Within hours I was having a violent reaction that lasted two days. Within a couple of months I had diarrhoea that just wouldn't stop. I went to the GP who prescribed medication but it just got worse. The pain was just unbelievable – it felt as if I was being stabbed in the belly repeatedly. When the bleeding started I was referred to a specialist. After some tests (which I would be in no hurry to repeat) I finally received a diagnosis. I had Crohn's disease. This is a condition in which the gut wall becomes highly inflamed. My uncle Harry-boy's daughter, Marion, died from a similar condition.

I was put on medication (Sulfasalazine) that made no difference except that it turned my urine fluorescent orange. Some public urinals for men feature a long white ceramic trough. If I were at the high end of the trough, the other men would look down at the fluorescent orange liquid flowing past them and slowly look around as if to say, "What the hell have you been drinking?" Nobody ever actually said anything, though. After many months without any improvement my consultant, in apparent desperation, asked me, "Do you eat much sugar?" If you ask 100 teenagers if they get too much

homework, 90 of them will say yes. Ask a 16 year old, "Do you eat much sugar?" and he'll say no. I said no, but decided to cut out sugar just to see. My condition completely healed in weeks. I subsequently read a book about sugar called, *Pure, White and Deadly*, which described the effects of sugar on our health. This really awakened me to the fact that health and disease are largely determined by what we do in our lives, rather than being predetermined. It also made me wary of doing anything that would damage my health again – good preparation for a career in the rock business. Six months later I was interviewed at medical schools. My negative experience with health and disease drew me away from that path at the time, so I went into the music business instead. I don't know if I would have ended up working in natural medicine if it were not for that illness.

According to the spiritual writer, Henry Nouwen; 'The Wounded Healer's own wounds are profoundly important to the healing process. They provide an awareness of the pain, torment, and confusion underlying any affliction.'

Anyone who is involved with healing in any way must be aware of the inextricable link between the body and the mind. Norman Cousins (1915 – 1990) pioneered a great deal of the research on this. He was a journalist, editor, peace campaigner and also a wounded healer. However, I will always remember him as the father of Psychoneuroimmunology, which is the study of the ways in which the mind can influence the workings of the body. At the age of ten, Cousins went into a sanatorium for tuberculosis. Whilst there he observed that the inmates fell into two distinct groups: those who were waiting to die and those who were trying to escape. These escape artists had a much better survival rate.

Thus, at the tender age of 10, the seeds were planted of an awareness that what goes on in your mind can influence your physical health. At 49 years old, Cousins' joints were rapidly degenerating. He was diagnosed as having ankylosing spondylitis, a chronic, inflammatory arthritis and autoimmune disease with various complications. He was given a one in five hundred chance of surviving. Whilst lying in a hospital bed he noticed something very peculiar. When he laughed long and hard, his pain would diminish and he would get

two hours of restful sleep before the pain returned. He acquired a projector and started watching comedy movies like those of the Marx Brothers. This helped his condition but disturbed the other patients, so with his doctor's agreement, he moved to a hotel room. This resulted in two changes – better sleep and smaller bills. His condition improved and he came back to health, surviving over 20 more years. He later developed 'The Norman Cousins Center for Psychoneuroimmunology' at UCLA. One of the most profound statements he ever made was: 'Words can kill and words can heal.' I've lost count of the number of times I've wished that all health professionals would pay heed to those words. So much damage is done to patients by the words of doctors. A common example is, "It might be cancer." Such a statement can not only cause immense distress to the patient, as well as their family, but also physical damage in the body. I feel that there's absolutely no point in discussing cancer with the patient unless there's reasonable evidence for it.

Talking of wounded healers, my old friend Nasty Suicide surprised everyone by making a transformation not unlike my own. He is now a qualified pharmacist. He still plays music, as he's a gifted guitarist. I was delighted to hear that he is happy and settled as he used to get a bit wild at times.

<p align="center">—◆—</p>

My first clinic was such a big success that I had to bring my brother Bryn in to help me run it. We decided to open another one but we had different ideas about it. He felt that we should duplicate our success by opening a similar place in a similar area, which would, we predicted, be successful. I had some sympathy with this view but I had been to Liverpool St station, which is situated in the Golden Mile, the one square mile in the centre of London where more money passes through than in any other city in the world, as it's the banking centre of the whole planet. I stood outside Liverpool St station in the rush hour one morning and watched a quarter of a million people emerge to go to work. I found out there were very few chiropractors within that square mile and that this was therefore a golden opportunity.

Property prices are understandably very expensive in that area but the economy was in recession, which meant that there were good deals to be had. I found a terraced house, five storeys high, which was quite big enough for a clinic but it was very run down with terrible décor and a leaking roof. The owner was 94 years old and told me that he didn't want to do a deal of more than five years duration, which was understandable. I said I would refurbish the building at my own expense but I wanted to pay £5,000 per year in rent, with the first six months rent-free. A crazy offer had worked for me last time so why not try again? The owner accepted.

Bryn and I compromised by going for both options. We eventually bought a clinic in Finchley, North London and opened the one in the square mile in 1996. I got my friend Mickey Daltry, who is a builder, to refurbish the building, including a new roof, for £30,000. Thus I was paying in effect £52.500 for five years, the equivalent of just over £200 per week. When the five years were up, I had to pay the market rent and was told by the new landlords that it would be £1500 per week - a 787% increase. At that point I sold the business. It is perfectly possible for a well-run clinic to pay £1500 per week rent but I have found in business that low overheads take the stress away.

Running three clinics was certainly very stressful. I now realise that running two clinics creates three times the stress of one and three clinics cause five times the stress of one. When I told this to my friend Sally Middleton, she immediately responded, "That's the same as children". Soon after opening the three clinics I met Dr Chuck Gibson from California who taught me all about systems in a chiropractic clinic and also a great deal about chiropractic philosophy. After spending time with Chuck and his colleague, Dr Jay Morgan, I understood very clearly why utilising the body's own healing power is so much better than trying to control the body with drugs. Chuck has been a long term friend and mentor to me.

New patients come to me from all sorts of different sources. Driving home from a night out I had a call on my mobile phone. A man's voice said,

"Is that Terry Chimes?"

"Yes."

"Is it the Terry Chimes that used to play for The Clash?"

"Yes."

"This is the singer."

Of course it was Joe Strummer because there's nobody else in this world that would start a conversation like that. He went on to say that a close friend of his was in serious trouble with his back and wanted to know if I could help him, which I eventually did.

Denis the dog was getting old and finding it hard to get on his feet. I tried everything I could but he was just worn out. The day came when I had to take him to the vet to put an end to his suffering. I took him there, said goodbye to that amazing little character with whom I'd shared the last sixteen years of my life, got back into the empty car and drove home. I've had some tough jobs in my time but that was the toughest.

LOOKING AFTER BUSINESS

My constant urge to help other people get better had resulted in my becoming a practitioner, but there was another way to help people, to which, I inevitably gravitated. Having been very successful in running a business, I had lots of calls for help from people who were struggling with making their businesses work. Initially these were other practitioners but later they were coming in from all sorts of companies. I formed a business club, which has been running for a few years now. We meet monthly and exchange ideas. We also support and help one another, as running your own business can be a very lonely life.

Looking back at the early days when work as a musician was scarce, I used my imagination and thought about how I could market my skills. I decided the way to market myself was to teach people to do what I do, which was playing drums. I developed a syllabus, sound-proofed a room in my house, and advertised. I quickly found a large number of people who were

happy to pay for lessons. One of the problems with being an active musician is that you can never do a 'proper' job, because you are always being called away to perform in different countries. The beauty of this situation was that the students didn't mind me disappearing on tour for weeks. In fact, they liked it, because they felt they were being taught by somebody who was the real deal. As soon as I got comfortable in my new teaching role, I looked for a way to raise my game further.

It occurred to me that all my students were continually spending money on replacement consumables: drumsticks break, drum-skins wear out, and so on. I therefore decided to become a supplier of these items; after all, I already had the customers. I simply needed to expand the range of services I provided. I purchased the stock wholesale and had virtually no overheads. As a result, with only a small amount of extra work, I had doubled my income from the teaching. As soon I got comfortable with the new role of teacher and supplier, I needed to find a new way to raise my game. I decided to film an instruction video called *Tricks Of The Trade*. It was intended to show young up and coming drummers all the skills I had learned the hard way. I got it reviewed by the music press and put it on the market.

The point is that by using your imagination and aiming higher you can usually go further. Incidentally, this was the first project that I carried out in partnership with my younger brother Bryn.

It was a similar story in my chiropractic career. I set up a clinic, that became a big success, and as I've recounted, I decided to hire some associate chiropractors to work with me, because with only one pair of hands there is a limit to how many people you can see. We soon filled up the building we were in and so I opened two further clinics in other parts of London. This taught me how crucially important it is to adequately train and manage your staff. By 1999 I had three chiropractic clinics in London and 26 staff. I couldn't manage all of this by myself but for some time my brother Bryn had been helping me. He is much better with details than I am. We have often joked that I would be in prison by now if it weren't for Bryn sorting out tax and legal matters. We have since embarked on many other projects together, along

with my older brother John, since I don't trust anyone who doesn't have the same mother as me!

Having faced these challenges and overcome them, I was getting too comfortable again. I decided to set up another company to consult with chiropractors and teach them how to run their clinics. Within one year, we'd become Europe's largest chiropractic consulting company, reaching fourteen countries. Next I realized that dentists face many of the same challenges as chiropractors, so I brought them into the program as well. We got so busy that it was difficult to find enough time. Then the Internet came to the rescue — we put everything online so people could do the seminars in their own time without leaving the house. As I started to get comfortable with consulting and lecturing, I found myself in need of a new challenge, which you will hear about later in this chapter. You may wonder why I don't ever appear to stop when I get comfortable, but for me it is the challenge that is exciting and there is no challenge in being comfortable.

As you look at people who have achieved what you want to achieve, you may find yourself asking the question, "What have they got that I haven't got? Are they better looking, more intelligent, or better educated than me? Perhaps they are just luckier than me." As someone who has coached hundreds of individuals, I can tell you that the difference is usually none of the above. The real difference is how they go about doing it. The whole world is littered with people who have great talent but didn't fulfil their potential. In a strange way, great gifts and talents can be a hindrance when you are young, because they get you into the habit of not trying very hard. Persistence, hard work and focussing on the outcome, not the obstacle, is what sets successful people apart. Whenever a person says, "I can't do that", they are closing a potential door to success. When I coach people, I can show them what is possible, I can make the steps as easy and small as possible, and I can write down on paper the results they will achieve. What I can never do is step into their shoes and do it for them. When I start coaching a new client I can rapidly identify how far they will go by their willingness to change and their persistence in pursuit of excellence.

I have given hundreds of seminars and had lots of funny experiences. I'll share here my favourite one. We once threw a post-seminar party at the Renaissance hotel at Heathrow Airport, London. I walked into the hall quite early on to find that there was a DJ, about 15 men and no women. Some of the seminar attendees said to me, "Terry, where are all the girls?" I said, "Don't worry, there will be plenty of girls along soon." Five minutes later the hotel duty manager came to see me. He said, "I really need your help." I couldn't imagine what he wanted. He said, "We have 300 air stewardesses upstairs in a party. The sound system is broken and we can't fix it. Is there any way that you could let them join your party?" I said, "OK, send them down here, but you owe me a favour!" I went over to the same guys and said, "I've ordered some girls for you." They gave me a puzzled look and one of them said, "How many?" I casually replied, "About 300." They all burst into laughter and then another said, "So when will they get here?" I replied, "In about ten minutes." This was followed by even more laughter and one of them said something about me having an overactive imagination. I then sat down to watch their faces as, sure enough, 300 young women who were dressed up to the nines, walked in. Naturally, when the guys asked me how I'd done it, I told them that it was an old trick I'd learned in the music business.

In 2002 I had an idea for the chiropractic seminars. I planned to have around 300 drums in the hall and invite the seminar attendees to pick up one each and play. I could lead the session and have them all bashing out simple rhythms. I was confident this would work as so many people have told me how they would love to have a go at bashing a drum. I called up Darren, an old friend at Remo drums, and put the idea to him. There was a long pause. He eventually said, "Are you taking the Mickey?" I was a bit surprised and asked what he meant. He said, "We had this idea about ten years ago and we thought you would be the ideal person to do it. We asked you and you said you weren't interested. Now you come back and tell me you've got a great idea!" Apparently they had been staging these 'Drum Circles' all over the world. I had no memory of that conversation but it would have been around the time I was taking two sets of final exams, so there would have been no way at that time. Darren was kind enough to help me get the 300 drums and it

went very well. My main memory of that time is that the guys with big egos found the biggest, loudest drum they could get their hands on and the shy ones found the smallest instruments.

DR TERRY'S ANECDOSAGE

Over the years I have treated lots of celebrities, especially musicians, but also top athletes, footballers, boxers and actors. I have never made any effort to go out and find celebrity patients. They just seem to find me. It's as though, because I have been in the public eye, they think I will be more appropriate for them than another chiropractor. Lots of doctors and therapists actively seek out celebrity patients and they feel this gives them kudos. I personally prefer to treat Mrs Jones around the corner as, having been around lots of famous people, I tend to see them as no different from anyone else.

My brother, John, had his tonsils removed when he was nine years old. Just before going down for the operation my father explained to him what was going to happen but missed out the grisly details. He said, "You will go to sleep and when you wake up we will all be here." John replied, "I won't wake up". My mother instantly said, "Lets get him out of here." My father insisted that it went ahead. When he got home he found that they had bought him lots of lovely toys to make up for the ordeal he had been through. I distinctly remember thinking, "Wow – getting ill is really good – you get toys". I didn't go down that path but I have met numerous people who clearly did and for whom being ill appear to be their main reason for living. That childhood experience showed me clearly how this could start.

Several years ago, a delightful eighty-something Irish lady was referred to me with a shoulder problem. She was visiting London for a week and had high hopes of me curing her as other family members had recommended me. When asked to raise her arm above her head she could only move the arm a few inches from her body. This is not a good sign. I x-rayed her shoulder and was disappointed to see that not only was the joint worn out but the wear

and tear had been going on so long that what had started as a ball and socket looked like one solid piece of bone. It would be very difficult to get even a few more degrees movement. I worked on her shoulder as best I could and told her to come back the next day. I expected her to tell me it was no different, whereupon I would reply that we had done our best but since there was no improvement we wouldn't charge her a penny and that would be that.

When she came in I asked her how her shoulder was and she pronounced with a big grin that she was cured and raised her arm fully above her head. I assumed this was the other shoulder so I asked her to raise the other arm. She raised the other arm above her head and said, "Oh, this one has always been fine, this one was the problem," and raised both arms above her head. At that moment you could have knocked me over with a feather as I was quite certain that what I was witnessing was impossible. As she was leaving she quipped, "My doctor told me it was incurable but my family assured me you could do it". I felt rather sorry for her doctor at that point. That case, along with numerous similar cases, taught me never to allow my conscious mind to put a limit on the body's ability to heal itself.

On another occasion an elderly patient once came in telling me how severe the pain was and how she had tried this and that to no avail. She said she had tried a vibrator but that didn't help either. I am 99% certain she meant a mechanical massaging device but it can be hard to keep a straight face at times.

One Saturday a man I had known for years heaved himself into the consulting room like Quasimodo. I think he had overdone some work in the garden and was really feeling the effects. He said to me, "I know this is ridiculous but I have to play golf tomorrow because I'm the captain. If you can get me to just walk around the course, albeit in pain that would be great." I told him I would do my best. He came back the next Monday morning looking decidedly more comfortable. I cautiously asked how he had got on. He broke into a big smile and said, "I won the trophy." Apparently he felt much better but was so worried about the problem recurring that he swung his club over a much shorter distance. The result was the ball travelled

in a straight line, and with his handicap, he got the best score. I have had a great deal of fun with golfers over the years because as soon as they realise that chiropractic improves their golf score they become far more diligent in attending their treatments and doing their exercises. Even Tiger Woods swears by chiropractic treatment!

The wonderful thing about chiropractic is that in most cases we are able to give patients good news rather than bad news and improve their quality of life. Obviously this is not so in 100% of cases. I remember seeing a patient who was forty years old and a fitness maniac. His time was equally divided between karate and squash. He was experiencing a mild dull pain in his hips and pelvis. When I looked at his x-rays my heart sank, as both his hips were completely worn out. They would need replacements and this would be the end of his karate and squash careers. I will never forget his face when I showed him the x-ray. He was so disappointed and upset. I am one of the most positive people you are likely to meet but even I was unable to say anything to make this man feel better. I have often been asked if over-training can damage hips. There is a great deal of argument about this in the medical world but I am a firm believer that long-term over-indulgence in high impact exercise causes irreversible damage. Having said that, doing no exercise is about the worst thing you can do for your health, approximately on a par with eating light bulbs.

I'm often asked why I don't get sick and tired of listening to patients moaning about their problems. The simple answer is that I have to do that because it's who and what I am. The urge to help and heal others is extremely strong in me. I only really feel like me when I'm helping someone. I especially like that first conversation with a new patient when they tell me what their problem is and how it has blighted their life. It brings up in me very powerful feelings of compassion, along with the urge to solve the problem.

When I see a new patient for the first time, I always put down my pen and look at them, inviting them to tell me all about their problem. So often the patient will remark, "It's so nice to be listened to for a change". This is because most doctors don't do it. They are afraid that the patient will keep on

talking for hours. As someone who has done this literally thousands of times, I can tell you that the patient will talk for an average of 45 seconds and then stop. They then get a happier expression on their face, their body becomes more relaxed and they allow you to direct the conversation. If the doctor interrupts the patient after 10 seconds, the patient becomes uncooperative and the consultation becomes longer and less productive. In fact with any human relationship, I have found that the best way to get others to listen to you is to listen to them.

I saw a lady in her 50s as a new patient. She'd had back pain for the last 30 years and had never been offered any treatment apart from pain-killers – a depressingly common presentation. The detailed history-taking revealed nothing remarkable or traumatic. I examined her thoroughly and found the biomechanics of her spine and pelvis to be very peculiar so I took some x-rays and arranged to see her the next day for the results. When I looked at the x-rays, I thought someone must have slipped some hallucinogenic drug into my tea. She had about 6 major fractures in her pelvis, which had healed up in mostly wrong positions to give the most extraordinary zig-zag appearance that did not make any sense. Now it is not unusual for a patient to forget about a car crash or a fall down the stairs so I expected her to come in the next day and say something like "Oh, yes. I forgot to tell you my parachute didn't open!"

To my astonishment she said, "No, I have never had any kind of accident, car crash, fall or anything else of that nature." Then she remembered one omission from the case history she'd described the day before. In her twenties she'd had an extremely rare disease called Guillan-Barre syndrome. This is a viral infection of the nervous system that causes complete lack of feeling that starts in the feet, creeps up the body, stops somewhere and then slowly moves back down the body. While the person is in the middle of this they can feel absolutely nothing in the affected area. She had long ago forgotten about having this disease but she did remember being in a hospital bed for many weeks. She also recalled that she had fallen out of the bed onto the hard floor several times. When the nurses came to pick her up and

put her back into bed she had told them she was fine because, of course, she could feel no pain. Clearly she had fractured her pelvis many times and the bones had healed in whatever position they had been lying. The good news is that we managed to get rid of the pain that had plagued her for many years. Incidentally, Guillen Barre Syndrome is so rare that the average doctor is likely to see only one case in their entire career and many have never seen one. I have seen seven so far – the odds of that happening must be somewhat similar to winning the Lottery.

I once treated a lady called June, a very independent tough person that didn't have much time for doctors of any description, but she had been nagged by her husband to see me about her migraines. She'd had them for decades and had given up on all the pills that had never worked. As soon as I put my hands on her neck I realized I could almost certainly help her because it was so very stiff and tense. After a few weeks of treatment her migraines had gone. To the casual observer this would be a nice but unremarkable story but I've always said that your health affects everyone you know and everything you do. I saw her husband sometime later. He was an old-fashioned straight-to-the-point kind of man but he astonished me when he looked me in the eye and said, "Thank you for giving me back the girl I married."

A patient will often ask me whether they should have surgery or come and see me instead. Many such people are looking for a guarantee either from the surgeon or from me. Of course, when it comes to health, none of us are able to give a cast-iron 100 % guarantee – all we can do is explain the risks and benefits of each approach and let them make their own informed decision. Norman is a retired GP I have known for years. He asked me whether chiropractic or surgery would be the best option. I explained the risks and benefits of both approaches and said that I was happy to treat him but as for the surgical option it was his decision. He came back in the following week and said, "I've decided to have the operation – it's nothing against you but I feel that it is the best choice for me. I'm having the operation next Wednesday." I said I respected his decision and would be happy to treat him as and when needed. On the Wednesday, the day of his operation, I was happy

to see Norman standing in Reception with a big smile on his face, saying "I've changed my mind." We have managed to keep him active and relatively pain-free for many years since.

I saw another patient in the same situation. He was a cartoonist with the largest newspaper in London. He had a couple of treatments with me and then decided to go with the surgery instead. Round about the day of his surgery a friend showed me the newspaper. There was a cartoon with a patient in a back surgery ward, the nurse was saying to the patient, "You've received a card from your chiropractor." The card had an image of a raised hand with the middle finger pointing up. Apparently anything that happens in the life of a cartoonist ends up in one of his cartoons.

Lots of people are surprised to see chiropractors treating young babies and children. They are also surprised to see us treating people in their late 90s. They may have seen a rugby player being hauled around the bench like a sumo-wrestler and assume that we behave in a similar way with a 90-year-old and a newborn baby. Clearly all these patients have very different requirements. Many people have asked me why on earth a baby would need treatment. The answer is that if a baby gets pulled from the womb by a pair of forceps, the forces involved on those tiny delicate joints are the equivalent of you suffering a severe whiplash. If your baby is crying and screaming all day and all night, it may be the baby from hell but it is far more likely that the baby is in pain and needs help. The good news is that babies respond incredibly quickly.

I see an endless succession of women in their late 30s or early 40s who have been trying unsuccessfully to get pregnant. It seems that if conditions are not ideal then getting pregnant is very difficult. Non-ideal conditions can range from emotional stress, chemical toxicity or the mechanical issues in a person with a bad back. The aim is always to find the stress and try and relieve it. There can never be any guarantees with this although a large number of patients have exclaimed, "You made me pregnant!" – an old joke that always makes me laugh.

I've always encouraged pregnant women to get their backs in optimum condition before the birth, in order to make it easier. Upon hearing this, most

of them ask for a written guarantee. The fact is that if you go into labour with a back that is weak, sore, inflamed and largely immobilized, you are quite likely to be laying there for 40 hours or more screaming your head off. On the other hand, if the muscles of your back are strong and well toned and each joint is moving like a well-oiled machine the birth is likely to last about two hours (this is an average of my patients over the last 20 years). Last year we set a new record with a birth in 45 minutes but I'm still aiming for the elusive 30-minute birth. I am of course never going to give birth myself but I just can't bear the thought of all those unfortunate women screaming in pain for 40 hours when they don't have to.

I have some patients that I have been treating for 20 years and obviously we get to know each other very well. They will often discuss issues or problems with me – not just because there may be health implications but simply because we have become good friends. Diane was a senior government official who I'd known for many years. She announced one day that she was thinking of taking early retirement but was not sure about it. She told me that if she retired she would be able to look after her mother who had cancer but would probably live several more years. I always try to be as helpful as possible so I asked a few key questions. I said, "Do you like the job?"

She replied, "No I hate it."

I said, "Could it get better?"

She said, "No, it's getting worse because of the cut-backs."

I said, "Can you afford to live on the pension you will receive?"

She replied, "Very easily."

I said, "I'm sorry if I've missed something here. There seems to be lots of reasons to do this and absolutely no reason not to do it."

She said, "The thing is, once I close that door I can never go back."

I replied, "You can never go back to a job you hate which will get worse and where you don't need the money – I suggest you resign today!" She did that and has been very happy since and was able to spend many precious

hours with her mother. It's so often the case that people already know the right answer when they ask for your advice but they need to hear it from someone else.

So often I am asked the question, "Is it my age?" Actually, the problems I see in patients are more often caused by lifestyle than age. I was concerned about my own spine after seeing so many people much younger than me with severe degeneration. I got one of my associates to x-ray my spine which I'm delighted to say is in almost perfect condition. I remarked to my girlfriend, "I have the spine of a 25-year-old." She replied, "Yes, and the brain of a 12-year-old." I was quite happy with that. A patient once came in saying, "I'm depressed today." I asked the reason and he said, "It's my sixty-fifth birthday."

I said, "That's alright, the older you get, the happier you get."

He said. "Is that true?"

"It's been proven." I replied.

He said, "Can someone tell my wife."

The reason people get happier (on the average) is that when you are twenty, you worry about what people think of you. When you are forty, you don't care what they think of you, and when you are sixty, you realise that they weren't thinking about you in the first place.

Brenda has been my patient for many years. She's the sort of person who has an extremely active life with complete disregard for her advancing years. However, she did tell me recently that she had decided to stop riding her horses because, although she was quite capable of riding them, in the event of falling off she might do more damage, as she was getting older. I was in typical male problem-solving mode so I suggested she should try riding an ostrich instead because if she fell off she would be nearer the ground and would do less damage. Keeping a straight face she said she would consider it. On her next visit she produced a photograph of her riding an ostrich. She told me with a glint in her eye that she had taken my advice. The photograph had of course been taken many years earlier on safari but she couldn't resist getting one up on my leg-pulling.

Sometimes I take on too much and tend to ignore those who say you should cut down and not do too many things. There was a time that I moved out of my flat on the Thursday, putting everything I had into storage. The next day I flew to Fiji for a week long course. I arrived back the following Friday, moved into a new flat on the Saturday and rushed off to a seminar in Paris on the Sunday. All was well until I arrived in Paris and my neck completely seized up. There were sharp pains in my head and I could not move. I needed a chiropractor desperately but the seminar was nothing to do with chiropractic and I couldn't find one. In desperation I got into a taxi and drove around trying to find a chiropractic clinic. Eventually, I found one – a very nice man called Francis. He was Canadian, which meant he spoke English, and furthermore, he was working for an old friend of mine called Phillipe Delite. Francis expertly adjusted my neck and the relief was so wonderful that I would gladly have paid him £1,000. I was delighted years later to meet Francis at many of my chiropractic seminars.

NEAR DEATH EXPERIENCE NUMBER 4

I met a very attractive girl at a party in America. After relentless pursuit I persuaded her to take me back to her apartment. We were sitting on a very nice roof terrace on a beautiful summer evening when the front door downstairs slammed. She jumped up like a scalded cat and told me to jump off the roof, as it was her boyfriend arriving. I looked down at the 20 foot drop and told her that wasn't going to happen and that we would have to deal with this guy. She gave me an incredulous look and calmly said," He carries a gun and he'll shoot you". In England we are not used to people having guns. I looked down. The ground didn't seem as far away as it had before. I clambered over, got a foothold on an alarm box and jumped the remaining fifteen feet with knees bent, springing like a cat. I actually managed this without any pain or problems. As I was walking away, she opened the window and shouted down, "It's ok, it was the guy in the apartment next door, so you can come up again if you want". I suddenly remembered I had a previous engagement.

I entered the 21st century with a bang – actually thousands of bangs. I was on the beach in Rio de Janeiro for a New Year's Eve party. The fireworks were amazing and we partied until dawn to see in the new millennium. Only months before, I had started a consultancy to train various doctors how to be successful in practice. They were coming from all over Europe to attend our seminars. This trip was my payback for all the hard work. Shortly after returning to London I got a phone call from my Mother. She told me that my father's speech had "gone funny." I got round to her in ten minutes. My father looked happy and healthy enough but he was speaking in a completely unintelligible way. I knew immediately that this was a stroke. We called an ambulance and they got him straight to the hospital. He came out of hospital some days later but with only partially recovered speech. We worked hard on trying to restore his speech but it was a hard battle. There was no problem with his attitude – he didn't have that reluctance to try that is so common with stroke victims. He just couldn't do it. The man who could do anything had finally reached his limits. His health further deteriorated and he had to go back into hospital. It was very difficult to see such a proud and independent man in that situation. I would go to visit at 7 am and find him asleep. Not wishing to wake him I would have to leave after 30 minutes without having spoken a word to him.

One day the nurses accidently cut him several times whilst shaving him. This enabled me to step in. I got the best shaving gear available and shaved him myself – very gently and carefully. This was therapeutic for me and, although he couldn't say so, I knew that my dad liked it. It reminded me of when he used to get me to cut his hair when I was a teenager. Eventually he slipped into a coma from which he never recovered. I was the last one to see him alive. We had pre-arranged that if he should die in the night the nurses would call my brother and he would call me. He called me at 4 am and we

arrived together at the family home before 5 am. I paused before ringing the doorbell, aware that the instant I rang, my mother would know her husband of fifty years had died.

But there was no use putting it off. Days later the funeral came. My brother John bravely made a speech. I told him beforehand that if he couldn't do it then I would step in. In the event he did it very well and I knew then I couldn't have – I was too upset. When a family of five loses someone it leaves such an enormous hole. With time we all got over it and settled down. It was soon after that that I had my life-changing spiritual experience in Brazil (see next chapter). I sometimes wonder if that huge loss helped me in some way to get to the point of that experience. The spiritual transformation certainly helped me get over the loss of my father.

<center>— · —</center>

When it comes to health and disease, there are some things that defy explanation. Here's an example of one of them:

In 2004, I went to a very remote part of Brazil to see a healer who incidentally describes himself as a non-denominational Christian. It wasn't that I needed any healing myself, I have mostly been blessed with very good health, which I am very grateful for. I read about this healer who saw up to 2,000 patients a day and I couldn't understand how anyone could do that. My research unearthed both positive and negative stories and I resolved that the only way to know for sure was to go and see for myself. I took a plane to São Paolo, then another to Brasilia, then a bus to the middle of nowhere and then a cab even further to my destination. This place truly was in the middle of nowhere.

One thing I found amusing about the place was that most of the deliveries were by horse and cart but they had a newly installed speed camera in the High Street. The healer's name was João de Deus. While I was waiting

to go in on the first day, an American said "Hello'" to me and then apologised as he thought I was someone else. The same thing happened with two more Americans. It seemed I had a striking resemblance to one of their party. Finally, the wife of the man approached me and said," I can't believe it, you look just like my husband." To which I replied, "You're a very fortunate woman". When I finally met my doppelganger, it turned out that he was also a chiropractor. He had come for treatment for polyps in his nose. When he reached the front of the queue, the healer put a pair of scissors up the nose of the chiropractor and ripped out the whole bunch of polyps, which had the appearance of a string of peas. A profuse amount of blood poured out of his nose, the healer pinched his nose and put his head back. When we came out of the healing place I asked him about the pain that must have caused. He told me there was no pain whatsoever, merely the taste of blood at the back of this throat. I asked him repeatedly over the next few days how the healing was proceeding and each time he told me that he felt no pain at any time.

The healer performed many other such operations and none of the patients had any anaesthesia yet didn't feel any pain. I didn't expect – nor did I find out how the healer did his work. I just needed to know if he was genuine, as it seems there are a great many healers who are not. I concluded that he was the real thing and had a gift that is, at the present time, entirely inexplicable in scientific terms.

Looking back on my time in the music business it seems to me that when I desperately tried to create a hit record I invariably failed. When I was simply concentrating on making the best music I could, I usually succeeded. It now occurs to me that this applies in life generally, not just in the music business. If a doctor spends all his time and energy in trying to get people better he will tend to have a successful practice, whereas if making money is uppermost in his mind, he will tend to struggle. This brings us to the need to have a moral compass in life. If you are wondering why I seem to survive all these near-death experiences and why I seem to meet just the right people at the right time, you may find some clues in the next chapter.

CHAPTER 8
ROCK'N'ROLL REDEMPTION

"Human beings must be known to be loved; but Divine beings must be loved to be known."

Blaise Pascal

Do you remember where you were at midnight on 31st December 1999? I do. I was on the beach in Rio de Janeiro in Brazil. I enjoyed it so much that I went back several times. I returned there for the Easter break. What happened there was to change my life forever. On the Saturday night I went to a party, sharing a taxi with a guy I'd recently met. We went past a church that was having a big parade, a long line of people with candles. I was feeling a sense of envy, that these people in the parade were connected to something they believed in, something greater than themselves. In contrast, I was there only for my own pleasure. As we arrived at our destination, I said to my friend, "It's not too late to go back and join that church parade." He laughed, but I was half serious.

Because I had read lots of books about spiritual matters and also practised meditation for many years, I felt I knew a lot about the subject – a fatal trap for anyone on a spiritual path. I had brought with me a book by the renowned Indian saint Ramana Maharshi. After being silent for decades, when he started speaking, people wrote down every word he spoke and published it. The format of the book was question and answer. One of his followers asked the question, "What is the significance of the crucifixion of Jesus?" Now this really intrigued me. I had been brought up in a Christian school and learned all those stories from the Bible. I had been in frequent conversation with God as a child. Around the age of twelve I had asked difficult questions about

Jesus and not been satisfied by the answers. Here was a man who was clearly a spiritual master being asked the same question. He answered, " The wooden cross represents the body, which is nothing. The son of man is the ego, which must die. The son of God is the spiritual part of all of us, which comes to life when the ego dies." This really got me thinking, trying to reconcile my traditional Christian background with all that I'd later learned.

The hotel in Rio had a roof terrace where I used to go to read. From that terrace you can clearly see the statue of Jesus on the top of a high mountain peak. I found it hard to take my eyes off that statue. It's so high that it constantly appears and disappears between clouds. I returned to England with a burning desire to find the answers to all of my spiritual questions. My thirst had become an obsession. I became quite hermit-like, going to work and coming home to read and meditate. I felt as though I was being led along a path. None of the things that usually interested me seemed to matter. This went on for about two weeks, during which I felt the answers were somehow coming closer.

Two years previously, in 1998, I had been to a car boot sale, where people buy and sell all of their unwanted junk. I don't like them but I stumbled across one when I was out with my mother, who loves them. The only things of any interest to me at these affairs are books. I bought about 20 books for a few pennies, and they sat on my shelf for those two years. I selected a book called, *Mere Christianity* by C. S. Lewis. The book was not an easy read, but it made good sense. There was a chapter entitled 'The Great Sin'. The great sin is pride, the tendency we all have to think we are better than someone else. I had always known that pride existed but wondered why it's referred to as the great sin. That was until I realised the significance of pride as an obstacle to spiritual growth. The problem with pride is that those who have the most see it the least. C. S. Lewis said that if you have done some good works, read some spiritual books, perhaps practiced meditation or given up drinking and you take pride in that, thinking that you are more spiritual than someone else, then Satan will rub his hands with glee, because he will have caught you in a spiritual trap from which escape is very difficult.

As I read those words I had the chilling awareness that I have been in just such a trap for twenty years. I put the book down and went to sit on the sofa. I was reeling from the realisation that I'd been in a trap for all of that time. Within minutes I was having the most extraordinary experience of my life. It's difficult to describe but I'll do my best.

I felt a presence coming through me in strong waves. At that moment, everything material and concrete seemed like nothing compared to the power and majesty of this presence. Everything in my world seemed to be instantly shattered, leaving me feeling tiny, naked and exposed. At the same time I felt the most extraordinarily powerful love. This presence knew everything about me and yet still loved me. The best way for me to impart how I felt is to imagine that you have the most amazing, loving father who always gives you everything you ever need and is always looking for ways to make you even happier. One day he's about to go out and says to you, "Do anything you want but please don't go into the room with the red door." To which you say, "Okay Dad." Later, as you look at that door, wondering what could possibly be inside, you can't stand it any longer and you open the red door. Inside is a table with a beautiful ornate cut glass vase. You pick up the vase and it slips out of your hands and smashes on the floor. At that moment your father looks inside and sees you. He doesn't say anything; he just looks disappointed. How do you feel at that moment? That's how you feel when your ego is exposed for what it is. When everything you've ever done is laid before you.

There were many tears, but also the most profound feeling that I would always be loved until the end of time and beyond. I also realised at that moment that my life could never be the same again. There was the feeling that all of the hairs on my head were standing on end and tingling, a feeling that has stayed with me on and off ever since. I decided to set about rearranging all of my life's priorities. The difference was that whereas before I'd always believed in a higher power, now I was in an intense personal relationship with him. When I came across the following poem, by Saint Augustine, it expressed perfectly my feelings at that time:

You made us for yourself and our hearts find no peace until they rest in you.

Beauty at once so ancient and so new, late have I loved thee.

You were within me, and I was in the world outside myself.

I searched for you.

You were within me but I was not with you.

You called me. You cried aloud to me.

You broke the barrier of my deafness.

You shone upon me. Your radiance enveloped me.

You put my blindness to flight.

You shed your fragrance about me. I drew breath and now I gasp for your sweet odour.

You touched me and now I am inflamed with love of your peace.

When I was nine years old I watched a film called *Trapeze*. It was a love triangle, with Tony Curtis and Burt Lancaster chasing after Gina Lollobrigida. Anyone who has ever seen Gina will understand why the two men were in hot pursuit. During the film both men kissed her very passionately. I was shocked by this and asked my mother what they were doing. She tried to explain by telling me that when two people love each other, they kiss as a way of expressing that love. "Kiss?" I said, "They're almost eating each other!" About a year later my hormones started working and I understood perfectly. The point is that you can be told something many times and not understand, but if you experience it, you don't need any explanation. Therein lies the problem of trying to describe spiritual experiences.

Have you ever seen another person engaged in spiritual activity such as prayer, meditation or using a rosary? To the outsider, these activities can seem very peculiar and somewhat pointless. Such an observer will be unable to see any purpose to the activity and may dismiss it as madness. I once saw a man blowing a whistle but it didn't make any sound. I thought he was wasting his time until a dog came running up to him in response – dogs can, of course, hear higher frequencies than humans.

So if you want to find out what this feels like we have to go back to the realms of experience, not words. To look from the outside at someone else

engaged in these activities would tell you nothing about what happens when these techniques work. It has to be something you do yourself. At this point you may still find yourself thinking that all these people following spiritual paths have some kind of delusional sickness, whereas you are quite healthy and don't need any of that. If this is what you think, be assured that you are not the only person to do so, let me tell you about a person who felt exactly that way.

When the writer C. S. Lewis was a student at university, he decided that there was no God and he would prove this to himself. He was studying literature and so his strategy was to make a list of all his favourite authors and then discover their religious beliefs. He looked into the beliefs of George MacDonald, Chesterton, Johnson, Spencer, Milton, Plato, Aeschylus, Virgil, Langland, Donne, Thomas Browne and George Herbert. As he went through the process, he was shocked to find that, after going through a great many of these names, he was quite unable to find one of them who did not follow a spiritual path. In the end, he managed to discover some others who were atheists, but he was distinctly unimpressed by their work. This was the beginning of the process that led to his becoming one of the greatest spiritual writers of all time.

<center>—•—</center>

In 2006, I was in Fiji, which is a wonderful place for a holiday if you should ever get the chance to visit. In one of the tourist places I visited there were some buttons on a plaque on the wall. I asked the attendant about the significance of the buttons. She told me that they belonged to the coat of the first missionary to arrive in Fiji. The natives had tortured, killed and eaten the man. This might seem a pointless waste of the man's life. But during the whole process the missionary impressed the natives with his gentleness and fearlessness. So much so that when the next missionary arrived some years later, they decided not to eat him but find out what he had to say.

This eventually led to the whole island being converted to Christianity. Those buttons are a testament that it is not the quantity of your life but the quality of your life that counts.

Some years ago I spent a little time in a French monastery called Taizé for reflection and meditation. The founder, Brother Roger, had busied himself during World War II helping people escape from the Nazis. After the war he decided to start the monastery from scratch, gathering a few fellow monks on the way. They resolved to build a church. They thought it best to plan ahead for growth and so gave the builders plans for a church that could house about 400, even though they had nothing like that number yet. There was a mix-up in communication involving metric versus imperial measurements. When Brother Roger returned from a trip he was horrified to find the foundations had been laid for a church big enough to hold 14,000! This reminded me of the Stonehenge replica story in *This is Spinal Tap*. He felt he had no choice then but to finish the building. While I was staying there that same church was overflowing with 14,000 plus people. Sometimes the inner voice is full of surprises. Sadly, Brother Roger was stabbed by a mentally ill woman and died at the age of 90 while I was writing this book.

In 2002 I spent a week in Taizé doing silent meditation. The idea is that you don't speak to anyone, which might sound peculiar but it tends to make you focus inwardly rather than outwardly. For the sake of convenience those in silence ate at the same time and place as those who were not in silence. I sat down to eat on day three and the lady sitting next to me started complaining about her neck, which was very painful. She said to her husband, "I think I'm going to have to go back home, I can't stand much more of it. It's too painful." This put me into a dilemma. I had made a decision to be silent for a week but here was a person in need. I thought it was no coincidence that she happened to be sitting next to me so I decided to temporarily break the silence and explain to her that I was a chiropractor and could help her with her problem. I briefly considered the possibility that I could sneak up behind her, crack her neck then run back into silence but decided that this would not achieve the desired result. When I had finished treating her I asked her where

she lived and she told me that she lived in Plymouth. I recommended she see Bruce Whittingham with whom I'd trained. He practiced in Plymouth and would finish the job. A year later I bumped into Bruce at a seminar. He told me that he had seen a very nice lady who had been treated by a chiropractor called Terry. He told her that he, of course, knew Terry very well. She told him that I had been doing a week of silent meditation in a monastery, to which he replied, "That can't be Terry Chimes, it must be someone else!"

All state-registered health professionals have to attend a certain number of seminars each year to keep their registration. I'm all in favour of this and would still do it even if I didn't have to. Most of the research tends to be a little dry but there is usually something interesting or amusing in each seminar. There's also a great deal of argument every time, which inevitably spills over to the restaurants and bars in the evenings. One of the most divisive topics is the role of faith and prayer in medicine and healing. It's well documented that people of faith live longer but, of course, the debate is focused on the reasons for that. Anybody involved in treating sick people will inevitably come across some cases where the patient just doesn't seem to be getting better. As strange as it may seem to some, I often feel that these cases are an opportunity to use prayer to help the patient, what's more it gives me the chance to deepen my own faith. Praying for patients has been extensively researched with remarkable results. There's evidence that tends to show that the patients get better. The surprise, however, is that those who are doing the praying have even greater improvements to their health. Plenty of hours could be spent in the bar debating that one.

People who are in touch with their inner voice find that their lives are filled with synchronicity. These are little coincidences that happen all the time. For instance, many times I have thought about a patient I haven't seen for a long time and they will suddenly ring up the next day, without me having done anything about it in the physical sense.

I recently experienced a really ridiculous coincidence. I decided I wanted a gong. I've always loved gongs. They make magical sounds and look fantastic. I will probably end up having a large collection of them at some point. Large

gongs are very expensive so I thought about where I might get a discount. I decided to ring my old friend Darren Bramley, who had been the rep for the drum company, Remo, when I was with Black Sabbath. Darren had supplied me with drums at that time and we became good friends. Darren didn't do gongs but I felt sure he would know a man who did. I hadn't seen Darren, however, for about eight years - when we did the drum circle at the seminar. I tried unsuccessfully to find his phone number and then I typed his name into Facebook. There were lots of Darren Bramleys and most of the pictures were of babies or dogs. After 20 minutes of searching Facebook I lost the will to live and gave up. I walked into the kitchen to cook dinner, thus missing a call on my mobile phone. I listened to the message and it was Darren. I was still in shock when I called him back - after all, it had been eight years! After our exchange of pleasantries, I told Darren I wanted a gong. A short silence followed and then he said, "How in the world do you know about that?" I said, "What do you mean?" He replied, "I lost my job three months ago and I have just taken a job as a rep for a gong company!" To cut a long story short, I now have a nice gong. But even though I have experienced this type of 'coincidence' for many years, I still get surprised.

Coincidences can sometimes lead you up the garden path, though. I went out for dinner with my friends Gary and Laura. We pulled up outside the restaurant in Gary's silver E-class Mercedes and I said, "Let me quickly go in and ask if they have a table free, as they're busy and there are no car parking spaces in view." I ran in and was told that there were no tables available. I ran straight back out and into the car. Slamming the door I said, "They don't have a table so let's go somewhere else." Then I realised I was in the wrong car. It was a silver E-class Mercedes, in exactly the same spot, but containing an Asian family.

I said, "I'm sorry, I seem to be in the wrong car!" They all stared silently at me. The whole family seemed to be thinking the same thing, "Don't say anything – it might make him worse." I then said, "I'll be on my way then, have a nice evening." As I shut the door, the car roared off. Then Gary and Laura appeared, having parked in a side street. They laughed uproariously

when they heard about my terrorising of a local family. I imagine that family keeps the car doors locked these days.

Pursuing a spiritual path comes with responsibilities. Doing the right thing is sometimes quite easy. The times when it is not easy are often those involving forgiveness. This next story illustrates the dangers of not forgiving.

A relative of mine called Ron wanted to buy an apartment within a stately home; a popular trend in England these days. He came across a man called Peter, who had recently purchased a stately home for conversion into apartments. Ron was very clear about what exactly he wanted: a large, grand apartment, with exclusive access to the main entrance. Peter readily agreed to oblige, although he naturally wanted a reasonably large sum for this and other privileges. The contracts were drawn up and the work began. Relations between the two started to deteriorate fast when it came to Ron's attention that one of the other apartments had also been granted use of the front entrance. Ron was livid. He insisted that he had been quite clear from the start about his requirements, and had gone into the deal in good faith. Peter argued that the small print in the contract allowed for some use of the front entrance by others. A protracted battle ensued in which lawyers were instructed on both sides. Feelings ran high and the very idea of forgiveness was far from both their minds. Then, within a few days of each other, both men suffered heart attacks. Ron survived his, but Peter did not. In the face of death, none of it seemed all that important. I tell this story to illustrate just how strong the effects of anger and bitterness can be.

Virtually every musician has a list of grievances. Most have had equipment stolen, promises broken, songs ripped off or contracts not honoured. It's easy to spend your whole life wallowing in bitterness, which many do. I prefer to think of the good things, of which there are many. The travelling, appreciative audiences, people you would never otherwise have met, the pleasure of creating all that music and sharing it, getting free clothes, haircuts, trips and instruments. On balance, musicians have a nice life. It's an oft-repeated cliché that musicians will find themselves lying on an amazing beach with a tequila sunrise, a beautiful girl and a gorgeous sunset and turn to

each other to say, "The careers teacher was definitely wrong." I've heard this myself several times.

I don't think Joe Strummer ever forgave me for quitting. Even years later he would deliver his long rant on the subject. It would always start the same way – he would say, "I woke up feeling great, the sun was shining, and I thought everything was fine." Then the rant would ensue and it would end up with him feeling depressed. I was looking forward to sharing with him my ideas about forgiveness but he went and died on me before we got that far. I fully expected to be sitting on a park bench with Joe, in our eighties, with him carrying on his rant and me telling him, "Isn't it about time you lightened up". But that wasn't to be.

The Baker recently pointed out to me that Joe had always been the one to fire people. He fired managers, roadies and even half of the band! When you are the hatchet man you don't reckon on being fired yourself. When you leave a band you are, in a sense, firing the band. I think that's why Joe found it so hard to forgive me, which is a shame.

I have always tried to forgive anybody who I felt treated me unfairly. It gets easier with practice. I have long ago forgiven the man who stabbed me, even though I never met him again. This does not mean that I would not try to get him convicted. He should be tried and, if found guilty, punished. That is all quite separate from the forgiveness. This may sound strange to some readers but forgiveness happens in the mind and heart of the forgiver, not the forgiven. The person being forgiven may not know or care if they are forgiven. My mother's father had been a drinker and a womaniser, which made life difficult for my grandmother. My mother was unable to forgive this during his lifetime but was able to manage it later on. Was there any point to this after his death? Absolutely – you can grow closer to God or you can hate someone but you can never do both:

To forgive is to set a prisoner free and discover that the prisoner was you.

Lewis B. Smedes,

One of my best friends from college days was a half-French, half-Belgian guy called Didier. We had been good friends for 12 years when he started to turn away from worldly concerns and follow a spiritual path. Just about the time we were looking forward to spending many hours exploring spirituality together, something very sinister happened. Didier became unwell and underwent a long series of tests, which showed nothing. Since we were both doctors, we hoped for the best but feared the worst. His muscles were getting progressively weaker. What we both dreaded was that this could turn out to be amyotrophic lateral sclerosis or ALS, one of the worst diseases it's possible to have. ALS is a form of motor neuron disease, of unknown origin, which causes progressive muscle wasting. There are no conclusive tests for it and there is no treatment. Eventually, the only visible functions that the body can still perform are breathing (just), swallowing and blinking. At that stage the mind is still fully functional, but is a prisoner within the body. It is this disease that afflicts the cosmologist and writer Stephen Hawking. When it became obvious that this was what Didier was suffering from, a group of friends decided to make the most of the time we still had with him.

We took him and his wheelchair to all sorts of places: churches, restaurants, nightclubs, bars, boats and planes. Somehow, if we were taking Didier with us, a visit to a quite ordinary place became rather special, as though we were all on some kind of mission. In later stages, when I visited him, I would hold up a card with all of the letters of the alphabet printed on it. I would draw a pointer along the letters and wait for him to blink. Using this method he was able to speak to the outside world. Amazingly, he would ask questions about what I'd been doing when we last spoke. I was so surprised that he remembered every detail about whatever I'd told him.

During this time, Didier's faith just kept getting stronger. To the astonishment of all who knew him, he never once complained about this most terrible of all illnesses; not one word of bitterness or anger. It's not that he didn't want to get better, but he felt that if it was his destiny to suffer this illness, then he had to get on with it. I found the way he dealt with it inspirational. I also felt that I had no business ever again complaining

about hay fever or a headache. I never saw him without being greeted by his wonderful smile. How was he able to do this? His connection with God just kept getting stronger and stronger.

If this seems strange to you then think about it this way. All of those people in churches who are praying or meditating are trying to perceive the reality that they are so much more than just their mind. Although they've been told this, their mind resists the idea by distracting them back into worrying about everyday things. In Didier's case his mind did not have that option – he couldn't do anything except look inward and explore. That is all he could do for all his waking hours. His mind was unable to keep up the pretence (that the mind is all there is) without being able to constantly throw up distractions, the way it does with most people. The peace and serenity that Didier found was astounding to see. It still amuses me to think of all the people who, on seeing Didier in his wheelchair, whispered to each other, "What a shame." If only they knew that he had discovered a level of happiness that they never knew existed. I know of more than a few rock musicians who could really do with spending some time looking inward rather than reading their reviews.

After nearly two years of worsening symptoms, he asked his parents to accompany him to church, where he received Holy Communion from his favourite priest (who happened to be visiting). He then returned home and died peacefully within minutes. He is badly missed by the hundreds of friends he left behind. To me, his whole life was a huge lesson by example, something that I, and many others will benefit from in future years. Goodbye Didier, my old friend. I thank you for what you taught me and look forward to the day we meet again.

In 2003 I started to take stock of my life. I had done everything I had set out to do. I was living the life I wanted, it looked as if I was going to be one of the last men standing as far as rock musicians go and it was time to ask the question "What next?"

CHAPTER 9
NOW HOW SHALL WE LIVE

"He that is kind is free, though he is a slave; he that is evil is a slave, though he be a king."

Saint Augustine

Upon my return from the French monastery, Taizé, I was greeted with the news that The Clash were to be inducted into the Rock'n'Roll Hall of Fame. I spoke to Trisha (Paul's wife), who was now managing the band's affairs, about the arrangements. I was curious as to what Joe would make of this. She said that Joe was delighted and looking forward to it. That surprised me a bit, although it was always hard to predict how Joe would react to such things.

Didier's death came just before Christmas 2002. I had the honour of making a speech at his funeral in Brussels. The day after Didier's funeral I was at work as usual with a hefty line of eager patients wanting treatment before going to work. I always keep my mobile phone on vibrate and that morning it just wouldn't stop vibrating. I sneaked out for a moment to listen to one of the many messages. It said, "So sorry to hear the news, will call you later." I listened to one more and it was much the same. I popped out to ask my two receptionists if there was any news, but they both looked blank. At last a patient came in who knew what it was — Joe Strummer had just died unexpectedly. I was shocked for two reasons. Firstly, he had been the healthy one — always jogging and taking vitamins. Secondly, I had always seen, in my mind's eye, the two of us in our eighties sitting on a park bench like those two old men in the *Muppet Show*, with him moaning about me leaving the band and me saying, "Isn't it about time you got over it?" I have seen a lot of unexpected deaths but you never get used to it.

At Joe's funeral there were lots of speeches. The one I remember was from Paul, the bass player. He recounted a time when they first knew each other, well before they had made any money. They were walking past a shop window when they saw some mirrored sunglasses, only recently invented. They agreed that they were really cool but quite expensive. Joe went in and came out wearing a pair. Paul told him they looked great. Joe produced another pair from his pocket and said "I bought you a pair too." Paul was pleased by the gift but was also aware that Joe would now not be able to eat for the rest of the week. This was the way Paul remembered Joe, a man with a kind heart. I hadn't remembered the sunglasses but I instantly recognised Joe in that deed, he had given me many things too. To me, and possibly many others, the public acclaim, fame, record sales and awards are far less important than the man's heart.

We still went to the Hall of Fame induction. There was perhaps the feeling within The Clash ranks that it was a sort of tribute to Joe. It's usual to play a couple of songs at the event. Apparently, Bruce Springsteen offered to sing for us if we wanted to perform but in the end it seemed that a video presentation would be more appropriate. Bernard decided not to come but Cosmo was there, helping everybody as usual. Johnny Green, long-term road manager came along to look after everyone. Topper decided at the last minute not to attend. Perhaps the shock of Joe's sudden departure, closely followed by a big party, had been a bit much. The ceremony is simple enough. Various people get up and tell the world how wonderful you are while you have dinner. Then after that they all shake your hand and say congratulations. That's about the easiest thing I've ever done. I was pleased to see Black Sabbath recently receive the same honour.

However much I change, I still love to catch up with people from my past. About seven years ago Julien Temple, the filmmaker who's been around from the first days of punk, made a film about Joe Strummer entitled, *The Future is Unwritten*. The plan was to have a campfire, something Joe had been fond of, and invite those who knew him to take turns talking about him to the camera. I agreed to take part and I was told it was starting at 11 pm and ending at 4 am. I explained to the organisers that I would have to do my bit soon

after 11 pm as I get up at 6.30 am. They assured me that I would be finished by 11.30. On the day I managed to finish at around midnight. I was walking back to my car when I bumped into Rocco Macauly our old photographer. It was great to see him and we walked back to the party together to catch up on the last 30 years. Finally, at one o'clock I left, only to meet Alex Michon who used to make the clash clothes. You guessed it – we went in to find out what we'd each been up to. Staggering away at two o'clock, I'd just escaped through the gates when I saw Keith Levene, who said to me, "Don't tell me your not coming in for a drink?" I can't remember the name of the person to whom I'd insisted on going first, but I saw him towards the end. He laughed, saying, "It's a good thing we got you in first, isn't it?"

Talking of my old life, a question I'm frequently asked is, "Do you miss playing music?" The answer is yes and no. I don't normally have time to think about it, but if I watch a band playing, I do get the urge to jump up onto the stage, push the drummer aside and take over! I have recently decided to learn to play the piano, which is more of a solo instrument than the drums. This puts some music back into my life and should also help keep my brain alive a bit longer (the principle of use it or lose it). However, regarding my drumming, I've always said, "never say never!" I will certainly always be a music fanatic.

In 2012, two Swedish writers who were compiling a book about various English rock musicians contacted me. I agreed to meet them as the project sounded interesting. The book was called *Keep Yourself Alive* – a reference, I suppose, to the fact that rock musicians tend to die early. They invited me to Stockholm for the launch which was to be a big party during which various people in the book could take to the stage and play a couple of songs. I thought it sounded like fun so I agreed to attend the party. Before I left England they asked me if I'd mind playing a few songs. I said I was happy to do that. "When did you last play the drums? " they asked.

"20 years ago! "

"Can you still do it?"

"Yes, it's like riding a bike."

When they picked me up from the airport they again asked, "Are you sure you can do this?" I assured them it would be no problem. When we arrived at the venue, I sat at the drums to play through a couple of songs and then I felt obliged to ask myself the question, "Can I still do this?"

When we started playing I found everything was exactly as it had been all those years ago and I played in exactly the same way, except that my arms were aching after a couple of minutes. I thought, 'Thank God all those punk songs are extremely short!' The party was fabulous; I met a lot of interesting people and spent the whole weekend in the company of other rock musicians who were featured in the book. We all got on so well that we decided we had the makings of a band. We have Dave Tregunna from Sham69 on bass (I'd worked with him in the Cherrybomz), Mick Geggus from the Cockney Rejects on guitar and Sulo from Diamond Dogs on guitar and lead vocals.

The four of us were sitting in a café in Stockholm and I asked Sulo if he knew what became of Susanne Blomqvist, who was married to Johnny Thunders. He said she lives here in Stockholm. "Good", I said, "perhaps we can say hello." Sulo replied, "Her hairdressing salon is nextdoor to this café." I couldn't believe it so I got up and popped next door and, sure enough, there she was! A bit surprised to see me, she left the poor client sitting there with half-cut wet hair to catch up with me.

The band met together in London and recorded a few songs and we seemed to be made for each other. I was reminded of the first time that the three members of the Jimi Hendrix Experience played together in a rehearsal room. All three of them said it just sounded right. It was the same way with us so we set about making an album. We call ourselves The Crunch, and the first album is due for release at the same time as this book!

This is the last chapter and I'd like to thank you for journeying with me this far. I've been asked many times about what I have learned in my life. If my experiences have taught me anything at all, it is this: Thomas Aquinas said in his great work, *Summa Theologica*, that men seek happiness in created things rather than divine things. Father Robert E. Barron cleverly summarised this into four: wealth, power, honour and pleasure. In my life so far I've had a little power, which I certainly don't want any more of. I've had more than my fair share of money and pleasure, neither of which bring lasting happiness. I've also had honour (this I translate in the modern western world to fame). What do these four (power, wealth, pleasure and honour) have in common? They are all forms of pride – they are all about 'me, me, me.' Spending one's life trying to acquire more money, power, pleasure and honour in order to be happy is like the alcoholic trying to get enough vodka to give him lasting happiness. Contrast that with trying to make others happy with love, kindness, mercy and charity. Then it's all about, 'You, you, you.' *That* is the path to happiness.

The little things we do and say in our lives can be much more important than we give credit for. The early years of childhood are filled with moments of truth – interactions with others – that can shape our future. Think back to your early childhood years and see what you can remember. You will probably find it's mostly a mixture of horrible moments and acts of loving kindness. Most of the rest gets forgotten. The point is that these little things are really the big things. I usually find that material things bring some good feelings but helping someone you love gives you a much deeper feeling, one more worthy of the name happiness. Furthermore, it lasts much longer. When you have practiced on those you love you may be curious to see if it feels as good when you help strangers. In my experience it does.

"If you want others to be happy, practice compassion. If you want to be happy, practice compassion."

Dalai Lama

The idea of contributing – giving something back - was something I pondered long and hard. There are lots of charities out there (I became well aware of that during my time in music) but you can't serve all of them at once. I wanted to use my experience and what gifts I felt I had to help those who were most in need. I also liked the idea of working for a Christian organisation. I met a lady called Clare Shinner who, at the time, was acting chief executive of the YMCA in East London. She told me that the aim of the organisation was to help young people develop in mind, body and spirit. That's why you always see a red triangle on the YMCA logo: the three corners of the triangle represent mind/body/spirit. That sounded perfect for a spiritual, chiropractic health fanatic like me!

I was asked to attend a Board Meeting of the East London YMCA with a view to possibly joining. I wasn't sure that I wanted to get involved but I went along just to see. There were 22 people on the Board (way too many people for one committee) and the average age was 72 – quite old for a youth organisation! I like a challenge so I decided to join and do what I could. Soon after, the Chairman retired and moved abroad and I stepped into his role, even though it may have been a bit soon for me. One of the challenges was that more money was going out than coming in, which is always a bit scary. The other problem was that the Board, having been there so long, was quite resistant to change. Various people assured me that it was impossible for this organisation to make a profit. My answer to that was, "Are there any other YMCAs making a profit?" The answer came back "Yes, there are, but they are totally different." I was not convinced. I managed to get the number of board members down to nine. We hired an interim CEO called Keith Drew and started a round of redundancies whereby we lost those who were not pulling their weight and encouraged those who were working hard. A year later we were seeing a profit of half a million pounds, which we were able to spend on improvements in the structure of the building and facilities.

As Chairman, I always tried to give a good impression in the local press of the work we did but we all know that bad news travels faster than good. Sometimes the news is unfair. A gang was chasing a young man down the

road and he ran up the steps of the YMCA in order to try and escape. He was stabbed there on the steps and later died. The headlines all declared that a young man had been stabbed and killed at the YMCA. Whilst technically correct it seemed unfair that this was someone we never knew and were unable to protect. Had he managed to get through the door we may have been able to help him. Being a chairman can be a tough job as the buck always stops with you. After eight years as Chairman, I moved on, leaving the place in a better shape, I hope, than when I found it.

You've heard many times the expression, "Giving is better than receiving." Well the truth is that giving is receiving, in a different and better way. When you give it away to others it is expanded, amplified and multiplied. Jai Namasivayam brought home to me. He is a Sri Lankan doctor who works at a local hospital in London.

Jai is a radiologist and has worked with me on various occasions. Jai was always acutely aware that whilst we in the UK enjoy a high standard of living, those in his country of origin are battling huge problems of war and poverty. Thinking it was time to do something about this, he started working on a scheme to build a hospice there. A hospice provides for terminally ill patients, giving them a combination of tender loving care, dignity and pain relief. The idea of a hospice in Sri Lanka was unknown at that time and people were used to dying at home in extreme pain. But there was interest among the medical community in this idea, as it had not been attempted before in a war-torn area. Having started work in 1993, the project finally became housed in a permanent, brick building in 2004.

In a strange twist of fate, later the very same year, that area was ravaged by the tsunami on Boxing Day, 2004. Of all the places that didn't need a disaster on that scale, the tsunami had to pick this one. Jai called all his friends and associates asking for donations. Most duly obliged. He went to the region within a few weeks to assess the situation. By April, a decision was made to open an orphanage. This was not an easy choice to make, as once you begin a project like that, you can't easily walk away. Another difficulty was that as children get older, having boys and girls together causes all sorts

of extra problems. Not surprisingly, most orphanages are single sex. However, some of the 25 kids lined up for the orphanage were brothers and sisters who had lost both parents in either the tsunami or the war. It just didn't seem fair to separate those siblings who had already suffered so much. Like most charities, the project grows in proportion to the need. This year they are taking on 300 more orphans. The commitment is to look after the children until they reach the age of 18.

There has been plenty of work and stress and, of course, Jai has not been paid a penny. I asked him if he has any regrets? He smiled and shook his head, saying, " It's the best thing for the soul."

People like to reward kindness but, of course, as I have mentioned above, as soon as you give you start receiving anyway. At least that's the way I understand it. That is why many like to give anonymously. There are those who say, "who am I to be rich, famous, beautiful or successful?'" The answer is, of course, who are you not to be? We also hear "Who am I to do anything about the world's problems?" If you think that you are not sufficiently important, rich, intelligent or whatever to make a difference then I would ask you to consider the next few pages carefully.

During World War II, London's East End was bombed, often several times each night. The lack of sleep took its toll on my mother who, at 15 years old, became ill with an infection of her spine. It was necessary for her to be sent away to convalesce for a very long time. Worse still, it meant going to a specialist hospital, which was many hours travel from her home. She was very sick and faced being away from her family and friends for about 2-3 years. She arrived at the hospital feeling frightened and a bit sorry for herself. She saw some awful sights on the ward, images that would stay with her for the rest of her life. The next day she received a letter. It was from her sister, Lily, who said that they all missed her and were thinking of her. She also said that if she was worried about anything at all then they were ready to help. That letter brought her a lot of comfort. When the postman arrived the next day my mother didn't, of course, expect another letter so soon since she'd received one the previous day. But she did receive another letter, again from Lily. My

mother received a letter from Lily every day for the first three months and then weekly for the rest of the first year she was away. My Aunt Lily was not a supermodel, a millionairess or a PhD but she managed to make a huge difference in the life of another person.

"If you think you are too small to be effective, you have never been in bed with a mosquito."

Betty Reese

I feel very lucky to have lived this long and to have had so many wonderful experiences. Writing this book has brought up an amazing flood of memories; it's mostly the people that you remember, especially those who are no longer with us: young Peter Lydon, Sid Vicious, Didier, my dear uncles, especially Manny, and aunties, especially Lily. Then there's Stiv Bators, Bill Aucoin, Joe Strummer and Johnny Thunders. Then, of course, my father, to whom this book is dedicated. I feel somehow linked to the millions of people who did me the honour of coming to see me play. Also the thousands who have had the confidence to trust me with their healthcare. I have so many fond memories of those I have coached and also those I have worked with in charity organisations. My life has had its problems and challenges, but I would not swap one minute of it with anyone else.

My job is very simple and very difficult. My job is to be the best Terry Chimes there could possibly be, just as your job is to be the best you that you can be. With that I wish you all the love, peace, magic and joy that life has to offer in all its splendour.

As for the future, I don't know what's coming up next and I'm quite happy about that. I know only two things; I will be working hard and I'll be helping other people. My main ideal is to see Dr Terry and Mr Chimes working together, maybe even happily ever after. So look out for more healing, more music and ... more books. Finally, my philosophy of life has been expressed perfectly in this prayer by Mother Teresa:

MOTHER TERESA'S PRAYER

People are often unreasonable, illogical and self-centered;
Forgive them anyway.

If you are kind, people may accuse you of selfish, ulterior motives;
Be kind anyway.

If you are successful, you will win some false friends and some true enemies;
Succeed anyway.

If you are honest and frank, people may cheat you;
Be honest and frank anyway.

What you spend years building, someone could destroy overnight;
Build anyway.

If you find serenity and happiness, they may be jealous;
Be happy anyway.

The good you do today, people will often forget tomorrow;
Do good anyway.

Give the world the best you have, and it may never be enough;
Give the world the best you've got anyway.

You see, in the final analysis, it is between you and God;
It was never between you and them anyway!

EPILOGUE

At this point you might be thinking 'where are they now?' So this is what I know about the current activities of the main characters.

Family

My mother is in very good health and still living in the house that launched several musical careers. Bryn is still working with me on a variety of projects, mostly on the internet. John is still playing in orchestras when his golfing schedule allows. They have both been with the same girls for over 30 years. My aunt Kitty is the last member of the family remaining in the East End where we all started. I was overjoyed to go to Katie's graduation at the chiropractic college, where many of my tutors are still lecturing. Anna is travelling the world with a design company – she helped me get the right design for the book's cover. Joe is currently DJ-ing in the Far East and loving it. Maxine went on to train as a chiropractor as well. She has now remarried and living happily in Northampton.

Bands

Mick Jones has had a personality transplant; going from a self-centered grump to the nicest man you could ever wish to meet. I asked him what happened but he just laughed. For the last ten years he has worked with Tony James in a band called Carbon/Silicon, along with various other musical projects. Tony James is happily married and living in Somerset. The song that wasn't a hit, Dancing With Myself, has been used in numerous films and commercials. Perhaps it was a case of right song, wrong time. Paul Simonon is still involved in music, largely with Damon Albarn. He is also painting

pictures. Topper is now 10 years clean and sober. He lives in his hometown of Dover and is slowly coming back into the limelight. He may even write a book (which would be a very interesting read for me). He and I have an unusual relationship – a bit like two men who have been married to the same woman but not spent much time together. We are planning on getting together to have a good long talk soon…

Bernard Rhodes still seems to be angry at the world – I doubt if that will change now. Sebastian Conran is still following his passion for design, Don Letts has been busy making music and movies. He also always seems to be the DJ at Clash bashes and still looks the same. Baker has retired to New Jersey, coming back to the UK only occasionally. Keith Levene has never stopped making music, Kosmo now lives in New York and runs a unique website dedicated to his (and my) beloved West Ham United. Alex Michon is currently running an art gallery in London. Wally Nightingale died in May 1996 from a drug related illness. Vic Goddard continues to write and play music.

I met up with Billy Idol recently. He's looking very healthy and still has a full head of hair (there is no justice). It was great to meet his parents again after 25 years. Anita Chellamah is still singing. She lives very nearby and is one of my dearest friends. Mike Monroe, Nasty Suicide and Andy McCoy have reformed Hanoi Rocks several times in addition to making various TV appearances. I bumped into Richard Bishop on an airplane recently – he's still managing bands from California – and I recently met up with Ken Lockie who has not lost his fertile imagination. Tony Iommi has had some health challenges recently but has responded by making a new Black Sabbath album which shot straight to number one. All of the multitudinous musical and personal disagreements from the past appear to be forgotten and close friendships have been rebuilt..

Chiropractic

All of my classmates seem to be doing well. Denise, my dear friend who actually had a baby during the course, passed away recently and will be greatly missed by all who knew her. David who started the first clinic I worked in has retired to Thailand. Clare Shiner who was my first CEO at the YMCA got married and moved to Australia.

In conclusion, those people from my past who are still alive are mostly very happy. It seems that you do, in fact, get happier as you grow older. I recently took stock and had a long look at what I enjoy doing and what I do because I have to. I decided that I love treating my patients, but running the business was work. Determined to keep to my lifelong aim to only do what I love, I sold my clinics but continued to work in one of them. This allows me to travel the world. Between playing music, treating patients, lecturing and writing books, I can see many exciting years stretching out before me. All is well.